THE JUDGE ADVOCATE GENERAL'S SCHOOL GUIDE TO THE **SERVICEMEMBERS CIVIL RELIEF ACT**

STANDING COMMITTEE ON
LEGAL ASSISTANCE FOR
MILITARY PERSONNEL

Cover design by ABA Publishing

This volume is published by the American Bar Association with the cooperation and agreement of The Judge Advocate General's Legal Center & School, U.S. Army. The materials contained herein comprise publication JA 260 of The Judge Advocate General's Legal Center & School, U.S. Army.

11 10 09 08 07   5 4 3 2 1

Cataloging-in-Publication data is on file with the Library of Congress

The servicemembers civil relief act guide
ISBN: 1-59031-815-3

AMERICAN BAR ASSOCIATION

Standing Committee on
Legal Assistance for
Military Personnel
321 N. Clark Street
Chicago, IL 60610-4714
Phone: (312) 988-5786
FAX: (312) 988-5483
http://www.abalegalservices.org/lamp

February 1, 2007

Dear Readers:

After years of debate and refinement, Congress enacted the Servicemembers Civil Relief Act (SCRA) in December 2003. The SCRA modernized, strengthened and ultimately replaced the outmoded Soldiers' and Sailors' Civil Relief Act.

The SCRA stands today as the greatest single statutory source of civil-law protections for American military members and their families. The Act's substantive and procedural reach is impressive, covering everything from mandatory interest caps on consumer loans to deployed individuals, to protections for military renters and their families, to the right of servicemembers to stay civil litigation brought against them during deployment.

The United States Army Judge Advocate General's School has developed the gold-standard practitioner's guide to the SCRA. This SCRA Guide is an indispensable tool for navigating the statute, for finding fast, reliable answers on specific SCRA topics, and for understanding how this complex piece of legislation operates as a whole.

The American Bar Association is proud to add the Army JAG School SCRA Guide to its arsenal of outstanding legal publications. The ABA Standing Committee on Legal Assistance for Military Personnel and the ABA General Practice, Small Firm and Solo Divison have co-sponsored publication of the Guide in the belief that every lawyer, paralegal and counselor who works with the SCRA should have access to this first-rate reference resource.

We are indebted to the Administrative & Civil Law Department of the Army JAG School, which produced the Guide, and to COL J.T. Parker, primary author, and LTC Jeffrey P. Sexton, editor and contributing author.

I am confident that as you work with this Guide you will come to value it as a constant source of reliable information and guidance for your SCRA-related practice.

Sincerely,

Earl E. Anderson, Gen., U.S.M.C. (Ret.)

Chair, ABA Standing Committee
On Legal Assistance for Military Personnel

PREFACE

This publication was prepared by the Legal Assistance Branch of the Administrative and Civil Law Department of The Judge Advocate General's Legal Center & School, U.S. Army. Legal assistance attorneys should find this publication useful in the delivery of legal assistance services to active component servicemembers, reserve component servicemembers, and their dependents. The information contained herein is as current as possible as of the date of publication. Attorneys should recall, however, the law is subject to legislative amendment and judicial interpretations that occur much more rapidly than this publication can be updated and distributed. For this reason, use this publication only as a guide and not final authority on any specific law or regulation. Where appropriate, legal assistance attorneys should consult more regularly updated references before rendering legal advice.

The publication contains summaries of the law, guidance, and sample documents for handling common issues associated with the rights and protections provided to military personnel under the Servicemembers Civil Relief Act. Sample documents are guides only. Legal assistance attorneys should ensure that samples provided in this publication are adapted to local circumstances and are consistent with current format provisions in Army Reg. 25-50 prior to reproduction and use.

This publication is part of the continuing effort to improve and expand the resources available to legal assistance practitioners. As you use this publication, if you have any recommendations for improvement, please send your comments and suggestions to The Judge Advocate General's Legal Center & School, 600 Massie Road, ATTN: ALCS-ADA-LA, Charlottesville, Virginia 22903-1781.

****

This publication does not promulgate Department of the Army policy and does not necessarily reflect the views of The Judge Advocate General or any government agency. As used within this publication, the words "he," "him," "his," "she," and "her" represent both the masculine and feminine gender unless otherwise specifically stated.

****

This volume is published by the American Bar Association with the cooperation and agreement of the Judge Advocate General's Legal Center & School, U.S. Army.

Contents

Chapter 1

Introduction

I. *Historical Background*

Military service often compromises the ability of servicemembers to fulfill their financial obligations and to assert many of their legal rights. Fortunately, Congress and state legislatures have long recognized the need for responsive, protective legislation.

During the Civil War, Congress enacted legislation suspending any statute of limitations where the war worked to thwart the administration of justice.[1] In World War I, the Soldiers' and Sailors' Civil Relief Act of 1918[2] directed trial courts to take whatever action equity required when servicemembers' rights were involved in a controversy.

A modern version of these laws, the Soldiers' and Sailors' Civil Relief Act of 1940 (SSCRA),[3] was penned on the eve of World War II. Based on the 1918 legislation, the Act provided for stays in civil proceedings,[4] interest rate reduction,[5] protection against double taxation,[6] and other types of relief.

Experience during World War II and subsequent armed conflicts led to changes, but the law's basic intent—allowing military personnel to give full attention to their military duties—remained clear. As the Supreme Court has said, this legislation benefits "those who dropped their affairs to answer their country's call."[7]

[1] Act of June 11, 1864, ch. 118, 13 Stat. 123. *See also* A. H. Fuller, *Moratory Legislation: A Comparative Study*, 46 Harv. L. Rev. 1061 (1933) (brief historical examination). In addition to the Federal legislation, many states enacted various types of protective measures. *Id.* at 1085. *See also* William M. Robinson, Jr., Justice in Grey: A History of the Judicial System of the Confederate States of America 83-8 (1941).

[2] Act of Mar. 8, 1918, ch. 20, 40 Stat. 440.

[3] Act of Oct. 17, 1940, ch. 888, 54 Stat. 1178.

[4] 50 U.S.C.S App. § 522 (LEXIS 2006) (providing that stays of civil proceedings when servicemember has notice of the proceeding).

[5] *See id.* § 527.

[6] *See id.* § 571.

[7] LeMaistre v. Leffers, 333 U.S. 1, 6 (1948). For a discussion of some of the early legislative changes and experience, *see* Robert H. Skilton, *The Soldiers' and Sailors' Civil Relief Act of 1940 and the Amendments of 1942*, 91 U. Pa. L. Rev. 177 (1942).

In 2002, Congress began taking a renewed interest in this legislation. During the 107th Congress, the Act was extended to members of the National Guard during certain periods of active duty performed under Title 32 of the U.S. Code.[8] Next, in late 2003, Congress passed sweeping, modernizing legislation when it adopted the Servicemembers Civil Relief Act (SCRA).[9] Finally, in late 2004, Congress fine-tuned the SCRA.[10]

The SCRA strengthens, clarifies, and modernizes the older SSCRA. While there are significant changes, most key concepts, protections, and benefits remain. Thus, much of the older case law—examined in this volume—is as relevant as ever.

II. *The Act's Purposes, Scope, and Constitutionality*

The SCRA provides a number of benefits and protections to service personnel. For example, it calls for the reduction of interest on debts to six percent for those debts entered into before entry on active duty.[11] Other provisions toll statutes of limitations[12] and stay civil proceedings.[13] The Act's stated, broad purpose, found in section 502 of the appendix to Title 50 of the United States Code, gives added meaning to these specific rights.

The purposes of this Act are—

(1) to provide for, strengthen, and expedite the national defense through protection extended by this Act to servicemembers of the United States to enable such persons to devote their entire energy to the defense needs of the Nation; and

(2) to provide for the temporary suspension of judicial and administrative proceedings and transactions that may adversely affect the civil rights of servicemembers during their military service.[14]

While not fostering any substantive or procedural right, section 502 serves as a guide for courts construing the Act. A majority of Federal and state courts construed the predecessor legislation and the 1918 version in a manner consistent with the Su-

[8] Veterans Benefits Improvement Act of 2002, Pub. L. No. 107-330 § 305, 2002 U.S.C.C.A.N. (116 Stat.) 2820, 2826-7 (codified at 50 U.S.C. App. § 511(1)). *See also* Lieutenant Colonel J Thomas Parker, *Soldiers' and Sailors' Civil Relief Act Now Applicable to the National Guard . . . Sort Of*, Army Law., June 2003, at 17.

[9] Pub. L. No. 108-189, 117 Stat. 2835 (2003) (codified at 50 U.S.C.S. app. §§ 501-596 (LEXIS 2006)).

[10] *See* Veterans Benefits Improvement Act of 2004, Pub. L. No. 108-454, 118 Stat. 3598.

[11] 50 U.S.C.S. App. § 527 (LEXIS 2006).

[12] *Id.* app. § 526.

[13] *Id.* app. § 522 (stays where servicemember has notice). *See also id.* app. § 521 (default judgment procedures and stays where servicemember lacks notice of the proceeding).

[14] *Id.* app. § 502.

preme Court's declaration that the Act be "liberally construed to protect those who have been obliged to drop their own affairs to take up the burdens of the nation."[15]

Although the Act benefits service personnel, it does not protect those who would abuse it. For instance, the Act "may not be employed to enable one who had flouted his obligations in civilian life to obtain indefinite delay or to cancel his just liabilities."[16] On the other hand, the Act forgoes protection in those instances where an "interest, property, or contract" has been transferred merely to take advantage of the Act.[17] Other cases have even noted that the Soldiers' and Sailors' Civil Relief Act is also designed to protect rights of individuals having causes of action *against* persons in the military service.[18]

The Act is not a panacea, however, for every legal problem of a civil nature a servicemember might face. It will not, for instance, help rescind a contract for the purchase of an automobile or a set of encyclopedias entered into after entry onto active duty. It is applicable to civil and administrative proceedings, but not to criminal proceedings. It does not excuse a servicemember from his/her obligations, but it will level the playing field so that military personnel are not disadvantaged because of their commitment to our nation.

> It may be granted that a continuance will probably operate at least temporarily and perhaps permanently to the disadvantage of the [non-servicemember] plaintiff. That result is unfortunate. But it is a reasonable exaction by society from one of its members for its own preservation; a proper imposition by the state upon an individual citizen in the course of its discharge of its constitutional obligation to "provide for the common Defense."[19]

The earlier protective legislation, the SSCRA, withstood constitutional scrutiny.[20] In *Dameron v. Brodhead*,[21] the Supreme Court found the Act properly based on Congress' power to "declare war"[22] and its power "to raise and support Armies."[23] The SCRA should be viewed in the same light. In fact, outcomes should not change with the new legislation.

[15] Boone v. Lightner, 319 U.S. 561, 575 (1943). *See also* Plesha v. U.S., 227 F.2d 624 (9th Cir. 1955), *aff'd*, 352 U.S. 202 (1957); United States v. State of Illinois, 387 F. Supp. 638 (E.D. Ill. 1975); McCoy v. McSorley, 119 Ga. App. 603, 168 S.E.2d 202 (1969); Application of Pickard, 187 Misc. 400, 60 N.Y.S.2d 506 (Su. Ct. Spec. T. Bronx County 1946); Murdock v. Murdock, 526 S.E.2d 241, 247 (S.C. 1999); Hanson v. Crown Toyota Motors Inc., 572 P.2d 380 (Utah 1977).

[16] Franklin Soc. for Home-Building & Savings v. Flavin, 265 App. Div. 720, 721, 40 N.Y.S.2d 582, 583, *aff'd*, 291 N.Y. 530, 50 N.E.2d 653, *cert. denied* 320 U.S. 786 (1943).

[17] 50 U.S.C.S. App. § 581. *See also infra* para. 2-8.

[18] Ricard v. Birch, 529 F.2d 214 (4th Cir. 1975); Ray v. Porter, 464 F.2d 452 (6th Cir. 1972).

[19] Bowsman v. Peterson, 45 F. Supp. 741, 744 (D.Neb. 1942).

[20] Following the Civil War, the Supreme Court found that "[t]he power to pass [relief legislation] is necessarily implied from the powers to make war and suppress insurrection." Steward v. Kahn, 78 U.S. (11 Wall.) 493, 507 (1870).

[21] 345 U.S. 322 (1953).

[22] *Id.* at 2 (quoting U.S. Const. art. I, § 8, cl. 11).

III. *Notice of Benefits to Persons in and Persons Entering Military Service*

Instruction on the provisions of the Act is required during an early period of military training.[24] Because this instruction is conducted at such an early stage, legal assistance and preventive law[25] programs should be designed to reemphasize the Act on a regular basis. Judge advocates should also endeavor to inform Army recruiters and local bar associations about the Act.

IV. *Material Effect*

As a final, introductory matter, it is helpful to pause and consider the concept of material effect. This concept is embodied in many of the Act's relief provisions. Simply put, regardless of the right or obligation at issue, it will often be necessary to determine whether military service has materially affected the servicemember's rights or legal standing.

This notion is best explained through consideration of one of the Act's key provisions. As an example, consider the provision relating to stays of proceedings when the servicemember has notice of the pending civil litigation.[26] When a servicemember makes an application for a stay it must "include . . . [a] letter or other communication setting forth facts stating the manner in which current military duty requirements materially affect the servicemember's ability to appear."[27]

V. *Purpose and Organization of this Guide*

This publication's main purpose is to provide guidance to legal assistance attorneys. It offers a starting point for legal research useful to military clients needing to assert a claim under the SCRA or those facing claims in an adversarial proceeding.

The SCRA has seven titles:

Title I—General Provisions (50 U.S.C. App. §§ 511-519);
Title II—General Relief (50 U.S.C. App. §§ 521-527);
Title III—Rent Installment Contracts, Mortgages, Liens, Assignments, Leases (50 U.S.C. App. §§ 531-538);
Title IV—Life Insurance (50 U.S.C. App. §§ 541-549);

[23] *Id.* at 2 (quoting U.S. Const. art. I, § 8, cl. 12).

[24] In fact, "[t]he Secretary concerned shall ensure that notice of the benefits accorded by this Act is provided in writing to persons in military service and to persons entering military service. 50 U.S.C.S. app. § 515 (LEXIS 2006).

[25] U.S. Dept of Army Reg. 27-3, The Army Legal Assistance Program paras. 3-4 and 3-6 (21 Feb. 1996); U.S. Dep't of Air Force, Instr. 51-504, Legal Assistance, Notary, and Preventive Law Programs paras. 1.3.1 and 3.2.2 (1 May 1996); U.S. Dep't of Navy, Manual of the Judge Advocate General ch. VII (3 Oct. 1990).; U.S. Dep't of Navy, Judge Advocate General Instr. 5801.2, Navy-Marine Corps Legal Assistance Program paras. 7-2j and 7-3b(1) (11 Apr. 1997),

[26] 50 U.S.C.S. App. § 522.

[27] *Id.* § 522(b)(2)(A).

Title V—Taxes and Public Lands (50 U.S.C. App. §§ 561-571);
Title VI—Administrative Remedies (50 U.S.C. App. §§ 581-583); and,
Title VII—Further Relief (50 U.S.C. App. §§ 591-596).

Chapter 2 of this guide delves further into some of the SCRA's fundamental provisions as well as into certain miscellaneous matters. Chapter 3 considers those protections, such as the provision for stays of civil proceedings, which can be thought of as procedural in nature. Chapter 4 turns to protections that can be thought of as substantive. Chapter 5 discusses taxation and voting rights and Chapter 6 describes the Act's financial protections.

Throughout this guide the abbreviation "SCRA," or the terms "Act," or "the Act" refer to the Federal Servicemembers Civil Relief Act, unless otherwise stated. References to individual sections are to the Act as published in the appendix to title 50, United States Code.

Chapter 2

General and Miscellaneous Provisions

I. *Introduction*

This chapter defines and identifies the persons protected by the SCRA as well as certain other basic concepts. Additionally, it discusses how and when this protected status attaches, the effect of this status, and, ultimately, how and when it can be modified or terminated. Finally, it considers some other basic concepts and points.

II. *Definitions and Applicability*

A. Basic Definitions

A discussion of the SCRA, like a discussion of most legislation, is best begun with a consideration of fundamental definitions:

50 U.S.C. app § 511

For the purposes of this Act:

(1) Servicemember. The term "servicemember" means a member of the uniformed services, as that term is defined in section 101(a)(5) of title 10, United States Code.

(2) Military service. The term "military service" means——

(A) in the case of a servicemember who is a member of the Army, Navy, Air Force, Marine Corps, or Coast Guard——

(i) active duty, as defined in section 101(d)(1) of title 10, United States Code, and

(ii) in the case of a member of the National Guard, includes service under a call to active service authorized by the President or the Secretary of Defense for a period of more than 30 consecutive days under section 502(f) of title 32, United States Code, for purposes of responding to a national emergency declared by the President and supported by Federal funds;

(B) in the case of a servicemember who is a commissioned officer of the Public Health Service or the National Oceanic and Atmospheric Administration, active service; and
(C) any period during which a servicemember is absent from duty on account of sickness, wounds, leave, or other lawful cause.

(3) Period of military service. The term "period of military service" means the period beginning on the date on which a servicemember enters military service and ending on the date on which the servicemember is released from military service or dies while in military service.
(4) Dependent. The term "dependent", with respect to a servicemember, means—
(A) the servicemember's spouse;
(B) the servicemember's child (as defined in section 101(4) of title 38, United States Code); or
(C) an individual for whom the servicemember provided more than one—half of the individual's support for 180 days immediately preceding an application for relief under this Act.
(5) Court. The term "court" means a court or an administrative agency of the United States or of any State (including any political subdivision of a State), whether or not a court or administrative agency of record.
(6) State. The term "State" includes——
(A) a commonwealth, territory, or possession of the United States; and
(B) the District of Columbia.
(7) Secretary concerned. The term "Secretary concerned"——
(A) with respect to a member of the armed forces, has the meaning given that term in section 101(a)(9) of title 10, United States Code;
(B) with respect to a commissioned officer of the Public Health Service, means the Secretary of Health and Human Services; and
(C) with respect to a commissioned officer of the National Oceanic and Atmospheric Administration, means the Secretary of Commerce.
(8) Motor vehicle. The term "motor vehicle" has the meaning given that term in section 30102(a)(6) of title 49, United States Code.
(9) Judgment. The term "judgment" means any judgment, decree, order, or ruling, final or temporary.[1]

Because of the SCRA's reference to other portions of the United States Code, it is necessary to examine more closely the terms "servicemember" and "military service" because both terms are integral to the questions "to whom" and "when the act and its benefits are applicable."

The SCRA makes the term "servicemember," equivalent to the term "members of uniformed services" as found in title 10, United States Code. "Uniformed services," then, "means . . . the armed forces; the commissioned corps of the National Oceanic

[1] 50 U.S.C.S. app. § 511 (LEXIS 2006). 2-3

and Atmospheric Administration; and the commissioned corps of the Public Health Service."[2]

The Act likewise defers to the title 10 definition of "active duty" to specify exactly what it means by "military service":

> The term "active duty" means full-time duty in the active military service of the United States. Such term includes full-time training duty, annual training duty, and attendance, while in the active military service, at a school designated as a service school by law or by the Secretary of the military department concerned. Such term does not include full-time National Guard duty.[3]

Simply put, the Act is applicable to members of the Armed Forces, commissioned officers of the Public Health Service, and commissioned officers of the National Oceanic and Atmospheric Administration when they are on active duty. It is applicable to members of the Army, Navy, Air Force, Marine Corps, and Coast Guard Reserves when they are on active duty,[4] but not when they are on inactive duty.[5] Similar language from the former provisions was found to be unambiguous. Retired personnel, not on active duty, cannot take advantage of the act[6] and neither can members of the reserves when they are not on active duty.[7]

As was pointed out under the prior legislation, the Act is narrow in scope. Under the former provision, several categories of persons related to the military were found to be outside the ambit of the provision making the law applicable to "persons in the

[2] 10 U.S.C. § 101(a)(5) (2000).

[3] *Id.* § 101(d)1. "Full-time National Guard duty" is defined a bit later:

> The term "full-time National Guard duty" means training or other duty, other than inactive duty, performed by a member of the Army National Guard of the United States or the Air National Guard of the United States in the member's status as a member of the National Guard of a State or territory, the Commonwealth of Puerto Rico, or the District of Columbia under sections 316, 502, 503, 504, or 505 of title 32 for which the member has waived pay from the United States.

Id. § 101(d)(5).

[4] As the definition provides, "active duty" includes "annual training duty." *Id.* § 101(d)(1). This is typically the two-week to twenty-nine-day duty that a reservist will perform. *See id.* § 10147(a). *See also* 32 U.S.C. § 502(a). In fact, the courts have acknowledged as much. *See In re* Brazas, 278 Ill. App.3d 1, 662 N.E.2d 559 (1996).

[5] "Inactive duty" or "inactive duty training" is the type of duty that Guardsmen and reservists perform during the traditional weekend drill periods. *See, e.g.*, U.S. Dep't of Army, Reg. 140-1, Army Reserve: Mission, Organization and Training ch. 3 (20 Jan. 2004). *See also* 10 U.S.C. § 101(d)(7). As to this type of service, the courts have also confirmed that the law is inapplicable. *See* Min v. Avila, 991 S.W.2d 495, 507 (Tex. App. 1999).

[6] Jax Navy Federal Credit Union v. Fahrenbruch, 429 So.2d 1330 (Fla. Dist. Ct. App. 1983); Lang v. Lang, 176 Misc. 213, 25 N.Y.S.2d 775 (Sup. Ct. 1941).

[7] Betha v. Martin, 188 F.Supp. 133 (E.D. Pa. 1960).

military service of the United States."[8] For example, a merchant seaman, captured and interned by the Japanese while aboard a Government vessel, was not entitled to the SSCRA's tolling protections.[9] Similarly, civilian employees of the armed services,[10] contract surgeons,[11] and employees of government contractors[12] have been held to be persons not in the military service of the United States.

The question of when and whether the Act is applicable to members of the Army and Air Force National Guards is trickier. This is because Guardsmen serve in one of three statuses. They may serve under state command and control and under state funding on state active duty.[13] They may also serve, as members of the federal reserve forces,[14] on federal active duty.[15]

Finally, they can serve, as they most often do, in the so called "title 32 status."[16] In this hybrid status they perform duty under the state's command and control, but with federal funding.[17]

Given the SCRA's definitions,[18] the Act does not apply to members of the National Guard during state activations or in most traditional, routine Title 32 periods. Likewise, the Act is not applicable to Guardsmen serving full time as Active Guard

[8] 50 U.S.C.S. app. § 511(1) (LEXIS 2006).

[9] Osborne v. United States, 164 F.2d 767, 769 (2d Cir. 1947). Ironically, the same individual would have been subject to court-martial jurisdiction under the Articles of War. *Id.* at 769-70. *But see* Rosenbloom v. New York Life Ins. Co., 163 F.2d 1 (8th Cir. 1947).

[10] Peace v. Bullock, 254 Ala. 361, 48 So.2d 423 (1950).

[11] Hart v. United States, 125 Ct. Cl. 294 (1953) ("fact that his compensation . . . was fixed according to the pay of a commissioned officer [did] not make him a member of the Army").

[12] Abbattista v. United States, 95 F. Supp. 679 (D.N.J. 1951).

[13] *See, e.g.*, N.Y. Mil. Law § 6 (Consol. 2003) ("The governor shall have power, in case of invasion, disaster, insurrection, riot, breach of the peace, or imminent danger thereof, to order into the active service of the state for such period, to such extent and in such manner as he may deem necessary all or any part of the organized militia").

[14] The Army and the Air National Guards of the United States are two of seven reserve components of the United States Armed Forces. 10 U.S.C. § 10101 (2000).

[15] There are many ways for the reserve components to be brought to federal active duty. *See, e.g.*, *id.* § 12302 (LEXIS 2006) (partial mobilization).

[16] 32 U.S.C. § 502(a) (2000) (outlining the annual drilling and annual training cycle for members of the National Guard).

[17] For a more thorough discussion of the Guard, its history, and questions of status, *see* Perpich v. Dep't of Defense, 496 U.S. 334 (1990). *See also* Major Michael E. Smith, *Federal Representation of National Guard Members in Civil Litigation*, Army Law., Dec. 1995 at 41, 41-43; Lieutenant Colonel Steven B. Rich, *The National Guard, Drug Interdiction and Counterdrug Activities, and Posse Comitatus: The Meaning and Implications of "In Federal Service*, Army Law., June 1994, at 35, 35-40.

[18] 50 U.S.C.S. app. § 511 (LEXIS 2006).

Reserve Soldiers and Airmen under Title 32.[19] It is applicable to Guardsmen activated under federal calls to active duty. It is also applicable to them, however, when they are in a Title 32 status for periods of more than thirty days in response to a presidential declaration of national emergency.

B. Legal Representatives

Along with the basic definitions, the SCRA clarifies that "[a] legal representative of a servicemember . . . is either [a]n attorney acting on behalf of the servicemember . . . [or] [a]n individual possessing a power of attorney."[20] More importantly, the definition of "servicemember" is expanded to include the servicemember's legal representative.[21]

III. *Start and Termination of Protections*

Although the SCRA's protections commence no later than when a person enters active military service,[22] there are provisions which expand this coverage. Reserve Component personnel, for example, are entitled to most of the Act's "rights and protections" on the date they receive active duty orders.[23] Similar protections would be available to those inducted into the service if the nation were to resume a draft.[24] In other words, protections under the Act may be extended and in advance of an actual report date. Furthermore, a servicemember is protected even during "any period which a servicemember is absent from duty on account of sickness, wounds, leave, or other lawful cause."[25]

The SCRA's coverage *normally* terminates "on the date the servicemember is released from military service or dies while in military service."[26] Other sections

[19] Decisions under the former law also came to this conclusion. *See* Bowen v. United States, 49 Fed. Cl. 673, 676 (2001), *aff'd*, 292 F.3d 1383 (Fed. Cir. 2002) (stating that active guard reserve soldier serving full time National Guard duty and later period of tile 32 period of annual training could not toll statute of limitations under the SSCRA).

[20] 50 U.S.C. app. § 519(a).

[21] *Id.* app. § 519(b).

[22] *Id.* app. § 511(3).

[23] *Id.* app. § 516(a). The "rights and protections" are those found in Titles II and III of the Act. *Id. See also infra* Chapters 3 and 4.

[24] *See id.* app. § 516(b). An individual ordered to report to induction is protected even though the induction process is incomplete. *See, e.g.*, Clements v. McLeod, 155 Fla. 860, 22 So.2d 220 (1945); J.C.H. Serv. Station v. Patrikes, 181 Misc. 401, 46 N.Y.S.2d 288 (1944); Ostrtrowski v. Barczynski, 45 Pa. D & C. 451 (1942).

[25] *Id.* app. § 511(2)(C). *See, e.g.*, Mason v. Texaco, 862 F.2d 242, 244 (10th Cir. 1988) (tolling protections extended to cover servicemember who "was placed on the 'temporary disability retired list'").

[26] 50 U.S.C.S. app. § 511(3) (LEXIS 2006). Diamond v. United States, 344 F.2d 703, 170 Ct. Cl. 166 (1965) (stating that release from active duty terminates period of military service, and section of Act which halted operation of statute of limitations during period of military service was not applicable after release from active duty).

of the Act qualify this "period of military service." For example, the protection calling for the stay of a civil proceeding extends for "90 days after termination of or release from military service."[27] As to default judgments, "[a]n application [to set aside a default judgment] . . . must be filed not later than 90 days after the date of termination of or release from military service."[28] Importantly, even when the member has left the service, the right to challenge the default extends for an additional 60 days.[29]

It is important to establish *exactly* when the particular protection ends. In a 1995 case, a former soldier waited two years and 1 day after discharge to file a tort action. The applicable statute of limitations was two years. Like the SCRA, the former legislation protected servicemembers by including a tolling provision. In any event, the court dismissed the suit, holding that the protection allowing for the tolling expired on the last day of the plaintiff's active duty, not the following day (the first day of civilian status).[30] In other words, the state's two year statute of limitations started to run the first day after the servicemember left active duty.

IV. *Divestiture*

The notion that the servicemember can be absent from duty but only when the absence is "lawful"[31] brings up a question about whether the servicemember can divest himself of the SCRA's protections. In fact, the courts have recognized this possibility. It has been noted, for example, that absence without leave (AWOL) is not "active duty."[32]

In a case involving confinement, an Ohio court held that a soldier sentenced by a general court-martial to five years imprisonment, total forfeiture of pay and allowances, and a dishonorable discharge at the termination of the sentence was not on active duty or service and, hence, was not entitled to the benefits of the Act.[33] In dictum, the court stated:

> I do not mean to infer that commitment for any violation of the Army's rules and regulations would divest the soldier of his rights under the Soldiers' and Sailors' Relief Act, but the gravity of the offense charged and the sentence of the Court-Martial are factors which must be considered in determining the question.[34]

[27] 50 U.S.C. app. § 522(a)(1).
[28] *Id.* § 521(g)(2). Despite the facial clarity of the provision, issues do come up from time-to-time. *See, e.g.*, Collins v. Collins, 805 N.E.2d 410 (Ind. App. 2004) (attempt to set aside default judgment twelve years after entry); *In re* Paternity of T.M.Y., 725 N.E.2d 997 (Ind. App. 2000) (attempt to set aside default judgment sixteen years after entry).
[29] 50 U.S.C. app. § 521(g)(1).
[30] Hamner v. BMY Combat Systems, 874 F. Supp. 322, 323 (D. Kan. 1995).
[31] 50 U.S.C. app. § 511(2)(C).
[32] United States v. Hampshire, 95 F.3d 999, 1013-16 (10th Cir. 1996).
[33] Mantz v. Mantz, 69 N.E.2d 637 (Ohio C.P. 1946).
[34] *Id.* at 639.

This reasoning was apparently applied in an AWOL case when a court held that a soldier who extended his leave sixteen days without permission to attend the birth of his first child, was entitled to the benefits of the Act.[35] Another court, however, concluded that a sailor forfeited his protection under the Act when he was AWOL during his divorce trial.[36] In that case, the sailor had been properly served, but subsequently went AWOL and did not appear at the proceedings. In yet another case, a soldier who was AWOL at the commencement of a divorce action, could not later reopen the default judgment by asserting the SSCRA while incarcerated in a county jail. The soldier's continuing AWOL status divested him of SSCRA protection.[37]

In addition to these cases involving AWOL and other unauthorized absences, service personnel may not be able to claim protection under the act if the true cause of their inability to act is misconduct such as a self-inflicted injury.[38]

V. *Waiver of Benefits*

Congress first added a section allowing for the waiver of benefits and protections in 1942. The current provision, found at section 517[39] is designed to induce servicemembers and their creditors to adjust their respective rights privately and to make it clear that no restrictions have been placed upon the usual right of the parties to re-negotiate an obligation.

That being said, there are a certain number of criteria which must be met if a waiver is to be effective. First, "[a]ny such waiver . . . is effective only if it is in writing and is executed as an instrument separate from the obligation or liability to which it applies."[40] Any waiver is only good if it "is executed during or after the servicemember's period of military service."[41] Finally, it is only good if written in "12 point type."[42]

While a servicemember might waive, in writing, certain benefits of the Act, s/he does not thereby waive all other rights under the Act. For example, when litigating the legality of a repossession, the servicemember does not waive the tolling of the statute of limitations as provided by section 525.[43] An agreement by a servicemember to waive SCRA rights pursuant to a divorce decree does not waive SCRA rights to any subse-

[35] Shayne v. Burke, 158 Fla. 61, 37 So.2d 751 (1946).

[36] Harriott v. Harriott, 211 N.J.Super. 445, 511 A.2d 1264 (1986); *see* Driver v. Driver, 35 Conn. 229, 416 A.2d 705 (Super Ct. 1980).

[37] Marriage of Hampshire, 261 Kan. 854, 934 P.2d 58 (1997). *See also* U.S. v. Hampshire, 95 F.3d 999 (10th Cir. 1996).

[38] Burbach v. Burbach, 651 N.E.2d 1158 (Ind. Ct. App. 1995).

[39] 50 U.S.C.S. app. § 517 (LEXIS 2006).

[40] *Id.* § 517(a).

[41] *Id.* The period of service extends for reservists from the date they receive orders to active duty and for those who are inducted from the date they receive orders. *Id.* § 517(d).

[42] *Id.* § 517(c).

[43] Harris v. Stem, 30 So.2d 889 (La. App. 1947).

quent litigation to enforce or interpret the divorce decree.[44] Such a waiver must be foreseeable, voluntary, and intentional.[45]

The opposite would, of course, be true as well. Re-negotiation, after entry on active duty, will work to reorganize whatever rights and protections the servicemember might have.[46] The protection, likewise, does not apply to obligations entered into while the servicemember is on active duty.[47]

VI. *Territorial Application, Jurisdiction, and Form of Procedure*

In general, the SCRA is applicable in any and every United States territory.[48] Its procedural protections, such as the protection calling for stays of proceedings,[49] are applicable in all civil and administrative proceedings.[50] They are not applicable in criminal proceedings.[51]

The Attorney General of the United States opined that the SSCRA was applicable to all agencies of the federal government. In so doing, he invoked the rule of construction that a sovereign is bound by a statute when the sovereign is a chief party of interest in the statute. He recognized this rule as an exception to the general rule of statutory construction that the sovereign is not bound by its own statutes.[52]

The courts have applied the provisions of the older legislation to the federal government,[53] as well as to state[54] and municipal governments.[55] Additionally, state courts have applied the Act in its entirety, regardless of whether a particular provision under which relief is sought has no counterpart in state law.[56]

Subsection 512(b) makes the SCRA applicable to proceedings commenced in any court within a geographical area over which the United States has jurisdiction. Section 511 defines the term "court" very broadly, thereby solidifying section 512's notion that the law is applicable to administrative proceedings and not merely the traditional civil court proceeding.

For purposes of federal jurisdiction, however, the Act does not generally present a federal question. In *Davidson v. General Finance Corporation*,[57] the court held that an

[44] Murdock v. Murdock, 526 S.E.2d 241, 247 (S.C. 1999).

[45] *Id.*

[46] *See, e.g.* S & C Motors v. Carden, 223 Ark. 164, 264 S.W.2d 627 (1954). *See also* Chas. H. Jenkins & Co. v. Lewis, 259 N.C. 86, 130 S.E.2d 49 (1963).

[47] Brown v. Gerber, 495 P.2d 1160, 1161 (Colo. App. 1972).

[48] 50 U.S.C.S. app. § 512 (LEXIS 2006).

[49] *Id.* § 522.

[50] *Id.* § 512(b).

[51] *Id.*

[52] 40 Ops Att'y Gen 97 (1941).

[53] *See, e.g.*, Edmonston v. United States, 140 Ct. Cl. 199, 155 F. Supp. 553 (1957) (Tucker Act); Berry v. United States, 130 Ct. Cl. 33, 126 F. Supp. 190 (1954), *cert. denied*, 349 U.S. 938 (1955) (Tucker Act); *cf.* Abbattista v. United States, 95 F. Supp. 679 (D.N.J. 1951) (Suits in Admiralty Act).

[54] Parker v. State, 185 Misc. 584, 57 N.Y.S.2d 242 (Ct. Cl. 1945).

[55] Calderon v. City of New York, 184 Misc. 1057, 55 N.Y.S.2d 674 (Sup. Ct. 1945).

[56] New York Life Ins. Co. v. Litke, 181 Misc. 32, 37, 45 N.Y.S.2d 576, 581 (1943). *See also* State v. Goldberg, 161 Kan. 174, 178, 166 P.2d 664, 667 (1946).

[57] 295 F. Supp. 878 (D. Ga., 1968).

action against a finance company for fraudulent conversion of an automobile sold at a sheriff's sale, following the company's foreclosure of a conditional sales contract, "[was] a common-law action for damages only incidentally involving a federal statute." There was no federal question, *per se*.[58] The Act likewise does not provide a right for collateral attack.[59] In *Garramone v. Romo, et. al.*,[60] a plaintiff asserted his rights under the SSCRA as part of a civil rights action under 42 U.S.C. § 1983. The SSCRA, while not a jurisdictional statute, may be effectively combined with other causes of action as an equitable argument.

VII. *Extension of Benefits to Citizens Serving with Allied Forces*

Section 514 extends the SCRA's protections to United States citizens who serve in the armed forces of allies.[61] The thrust of this section is to allow those persons who serve in the armed forces of nations that are allied with the United States in the prosecution of a war against a common enemy to receive the protective features of the act to the same extent as those who serve in the United States armed forces.

The protections terminate when the person is discharged or otherwise "release[d] from such service."[62] Unlike the former provisions, there is no mention of the characterization of service. The former SSCRA required the service be better than dishonorable.[63] Moreover, for certain benefits, the service requirement needed to be nothing less than honorable.[64]

VIII. *Transfers to Take Advantage of the Act*

Section 581[65] is designed to prevent abuse of the Act by servicemembers and civilians alike. It prevents the transfer of property from a non-servicemember debtor to a servicemember so that the servicemember may invoke the SCRA and prevent a creditor from obtaining relief.

The pivotal issue in the few decisions interpreting this section concerns evidence of intent to delay or defeat the enforcement of rights.[66] Consider the rather obvious, if not egregious, example of a defendant corporation that transferred a deed

[58] *Id. See also* 28 U.S.C. § 1331 (2000).
[59] Shatswell v. Shatswell, 758 F.Supp. 662 (D. Kan. 1991). *See also* Scheidigg v. Dep't of Air Force, 715 F. Supp. 11 (D. N.H. 1989), *aff'd*, 915 F.2d 1558 (1st Cir. 1990).
[60] 94 F.3d 1446 (10th Cir. 1996).
[61] 50 U.S.C.S. app. § 514 (LEXIS 2006).
[62] *Id.*
[63] *Id.*
[64] *Id.* § 572.
[65] *Id.* app. § 581.
[66] *See, e.g.*, Lima Oil & Gas Co. v. Pritchard, 92 Okla. 113, 117, 218 Pac. 863 (1923) (1918 Act); Sullivan v. State Bar, 28 Cal.2d 488, 495, 170 P.2d 888, 892 (1946) (evidence insufficient to establish a wrongful purpose).

to one of its officers on the day the officer entered military service.[67] Under those circumstances, the court had little difficulty denying protection that might have otherwise been available to the servicemember.[68] Section 581 clearly emphasizes the Act's equitable nature.

IX. *Missing and Deceased Persons*

The SCRA makes provision for servicemembers who enter into a missing status. For purposes of the SCRA's benefits and protections, "[a] servicemember who has been reported missing is presumed to continue in service until accounted for."[69] To understand the exact nature of this provision, it is helpful to begin with a consideration of what is meant by the term "missing."

Within the greater scheme of Veterans' legislation, there are two primary statutes dealing with missing service personnel. The first of these is the Missing Person's Act.[70] Because this law is referenced elsewhere in the SCRA,[71] it is the relevant legislation.[72] In any event, servicemembers will, under normal circumstances, be accounted for as present for duty, on leave, or absent without leave.[73] The Missing Persons Act, however, provides a rough definition of what constitutes a "missing status." Within that category, servicemembers may be "missing," "missing in action," "interned in a foreign country," "captured, beleaguered, or besieged by a hostile force," or otherwise "detained in a foreign country against his will."[74]

The SCRA's concern, as a practical matter, is not with most of these subcategories. If a command is able to determine that a servicemember is detained in a foreign country, then the benefits, protections, and responsibilities of the SCRA are as they

[67] Ninth Fed. Sav. & Loan Ass'n v. Parkway West Corp., 182 Misc. 919, 48 N.Y.S.2d 762 (Sup. Ct. 1943).
[68] *Id.*
[69] 50 U.S.C. app. § 582(c) (LEXIS 2005).
[70] The current version of this legislation is codified at 37 U.S.C.S. §§ 551-59 (LEXIS 2006). *See also* 5 U.S.C. §§ 5561-69 (civilian personnel).
[71] *See* 50 U.S.C. app. § 592.
[72] The other potentially relevant legislation is the Missing Service Personnel Act of 1995. This law was passed as part of The National Defense Authorization Act for Fiscal Year 1996. *See* 10 U.S.C.S. §§ 1501-1513 (LEXIS 2006). Ironically, the main gist of this legislation is to insure that missing service personnel are reported and accounted for whereas the Missing Persons Act is designed to insure that missing service personnel continue to receive pay and allowances until it is determined that they have been killed. This debate is of little practical consequence, however, as both laws necessitate that the servicemember be accounted for. *See, e.g.*, 37 U.S.C. § 556(a). *See also* 10 U.S.C. § 1501. For a thorough discussion of this area of the law, *see* Major Pamela M. Stahl, *The New Legislation on Department of Defense Personnel Missing as a Result of Hostile Action*, 152 MIL. L. REV. 75 (1996).
[73] 37 U.S.C. § 551(2).
[74] *Id.* § 551(2).

would otherwise be. If the servicemember is deceased, then most of the benefits, protections, and issues come to an end. The SCRA is obviously concerned with those servicemembers whose whereabouts are uncertain. For those who are truly missing, the protections of the Act are available until a more certain determination is made.

The SCRA also provides for deceased servicemembers. For SCRA purposes, "[a] requirement under [the SCRA] that begins or ends with the death of a servicemember does not begin or end until the servicemember's death is reported to, or determined by, the Secretary concerned or by a court of competent jurisdiction."[75]

Again, the Missing Persons Act is helpful. It confirms that the secretary concerned must formally continue a person in a missing status or "make a finding of death."[76] In other words, the Missing Persons Act confirms that the SCRA's concern is to only move forward when there has been a satisfactory conclusion that the servicemember is in fact deceased. The open question is the meaning of the phrase "requirement . . . that begins or ends with the death of a servicemember." The SCRA refers to death in two other sections. First, when a servicemember assigns a life insurance policy to another person, that person cannot exercise any option with respect to that policy until after the servicemember's period of military service.[77] The death of a servicemember would of course allow the assignee to exercise his options.[78] Second, the death of a servicemember will have an impact on the liability of professional liability carriers[79] and on "the requirement for the grant or continuance of a stay in any civil or administrative action" involving a professional liability claim against a servicemember whose professional liability coverage has been suspended.[80]

The "requirement" language probably works in a broader sense as well. Other "requirements" the law might impose, such as that to stay a proceeding[81] or to toll the running of a statute of limitations,[82] would cease to have any logical need for consideration upon the death of the involved servicemember.

X. *Insurance*

Three portions of the SCRA relate to life insurance, health insurance, and professional liability protection. There is little controversy surrounding any of these provisions.

A. Life Insurance

The SCRA's Title IV provides a means by which a servicemember may have the Department of Veterans Affairs (VA) guarantee payment of premiums on certain types of

[75] 50 U.S.C. app. § 592.
[76] 37 U.S.C. § 555(a).
[77] 50 U.S.C. app. § 536(a).
[78] *Id.* app. § 536(b). For a further discussion of the assignment protection, *see infra* para. 2-10a(4).
[79] *Id.* app. § 593(h)(2).
[80] *Id.* app. § 593(h)(1).
[81] *Id.* app. § 522.
[82] *Id.* app. § 526.

commercial life insurance policies.[83] Relatively few servicemembers have applied for benefits under these sections, probably because the law merely provides for a moratorium on premiums and does not relieve the servicemember from liability for repayment of the premiums.

1. Life Insurance in General

The SCRA's life insurance provisions are designed to provide a means by which any person entering the armed services may apply for continued protection by commercial life insurance. Upon proper application,[84] a servicemember may have the premiums and interest for certain types of commercial life insurance guaranteed for his/her "period of military service and for two years thereafter."[85]

The Secretary of Veterans Affairs is charged with supervising the implementation of these provisions. Section 548[86] authorizes and directs the Secretary of Veterans Affairs to promulgate regulations and procedures necessary to implement this portion of the SCRA. Pursuant to this authority, the administrator has prescribed regulations in volume 38 of the Code of Federal Regulations, Part 7.

2. Application

The provisions of the sections apply to commercial life insurance policies taken out by any person in the military service of the United States[87] "whose life is insured under the policy."[88] The policy must be in force on a premium paying basis at the time the service member applies for benefits. The servicemember must have taken out the policy and paid one premium not less than 180 days before the date the insured entered military service.[89] Also, "the total amount of life insurance coverage protection . . . may not exceed $250,000, or an amount equal to the Servicemember's Group Life Insurance maximum limit, whichever is greater, regardless of the number of policies submitted."[90]

Attorneys should examine policy provisions to determine eligibility. A policy containing a provision that limits or eliminates liability for death arising from or in connection with military service, or any activity that the insured may be called upon to perform in connection with his military service, is not eligible for protection under the Act.[91] A

[83] *Id.* app. § 547(a).
[84] *Id.* §§ 543, 544. *See also* 38 C.F.R. § 7.4 (2004).
[85] 50 U.S.C. app. § 544 (c). *See also* 38 C.F.R. § 7.6.
[86] 50 U.S.C. app. § 548.
[87] *See id.* app. § 511(2) for a definition of "military service."
[88] *Id.* § 541(3).
[89] *Id.* app. § 541(1)(B).
[90] *Id.* app. § 542(c).
[91] *Id.* app. § 541(1)(A). This relates only to the primary death benefit. If a provision limits or eliminates some other benefit, such as double indemnity, the policy will still qualify. 38 C.F.R. § 7.3(a). The insured may opt to continue coverage of those other benefits. *Id.* § 7.6(b).

policy that requires the insured servicemember to pay an additional premium because of military service is also outside the purview of the Act.[92] In fact, to qualify, the policy "may not limit or restrict coverage for any activity required by military service."[93]

3. Nature and Extent of Life Insurance Benefit

An individual entitled to the benefits of the Act may request governmental guarantee of premiums by filing Veterans Affairs Form 29-380[94] with his/her insurance company and forwarding a copy of the application to the VA.[95] The VA will then determine whether the policy is covered.[96] The VA's decision "[is] subject to review on appeal to the Board of Veterans' Appeals and subject to judicial review only as provided in chapter 72 of [title 38]."[97]

Unlike several other SCRA provisions, the insurance protections require no showing of material effect. Any person in military service may apply for relief in accordance with these sections. Relief may be granted regardless of the impact of military service on the individual's ability to pay the premiums.

Once the VA approves a policy for coverage, the "policy . . . shall not lapse, or otherwise terminate, or be forfeited for the nonpayment of a premium, or interest or indebtedness on a premium, after the date on which the application for protection is received by the Secretary."[98] During this period, the government does not pay the premiums for the service member but simply guarantees that the premiums will be paid at the end of the period.[99]

The insured servicemember must repay the unpaid premiums and interest no later than two years after the expiration of his/her term of military service.[100] If he/she fails to pay these amounts by the end of this two-year period, the amount then due is "treated by the insurer as a loan on the policy."[101] This assumes that the policy has a sufficient cash surrender value to cover the amount of the unpaid premiums and interest. If the cash surrender value of the policy is less than the amount owed, the insurance company may terminate the policy and the United States will pay the insurance company

[92] 50 U.S.C. app. § 541(1)(A).

[93] *Id.* app. § 541(1)(A)(ii).

[94] U.S. Dep't of Veterans Affairs, VA Life Insurance Programs for Veterans and Servicemembers Handbook (2006), *available at* http://www.insurance.va.gov/inForceGliSite/GLIhandbook/glibooklet.htm (last visited March 6, 2006).

[95] 38 C.F.R. § 7.5(a).

[96] 50 U.S.C. app. § 544(a).

[97] *Id.* app. § 549. *See also* 38 U.S.C. §§ 7101-11 (2000) (Board of Veterans' Appeals); *id.* §§ 7251-7299 (Court of Appeals for Veterans Claims).

[98] 50 U.S.C. app. § 544(b).

[99] *Id.* app. § 547(a).

[100] *Id. See also* 38 C.F.R. § 7.6.

[101] 50 U.S.C. app. § 547(a).

the difference between the cash surrender value and the amount of the then outstanding debt.[102] Also, if the policy matures as a result of death or by any other means during the protected period, the insurance company is required to deduct from the amount of the settlement the unpaid premiums and interest that were guaranteed by the VA.[103]

If the United States is required to pay any amount to an insurance company under the provisions of Article IV, the amount paid becomes a debt due the United States. This amount may be deducted from any other amounts due the insured by the United States.[104] Such a debt may not be discharged in bankruptcy.[105] Additionally, if the policy pays dividends, they may not be paid "[w]hile [the] policy is protected"[106] without VA approval. Instead, the premiums are "added to the value of the policy to be used as a credit when final settlement is made with the insurer."[107]

4. Assignment of Life Insurance Policies.

Title III of the SCRA provides a number of benefits to servicemembers. For instance, it sets forth the rules governing the circumstances under which a servicemember may be evicted.[108] An additional Title III protection involves the assignment of life insurance policies.[109] It is designed to govern the situation where, prior to entry into military service, an insured has assigned his/her life insurance policy as collateral for a loan. After entry on active duty, this section prohibits the assignee from exercising any right or option under the assignment of the policy "without a court order."[110] The need for a court order is typical of the other Title III protections and is required in this instance unless the servicemember consents in writing, or "the premiums on the policy are due and unpaid," or the servicemember dies.[111]

The purpose of this section is to require creditors holding life insurance policies as collateral to obtain court approval before attaching the proceeds of the policy. Resort to any remedy without a court order, or in the absence of one of the other three exceptions, can result in a criminal penalty and "consequential or punitive damages."[112]

[102] *Id.*
[103] *Id.* app. § 546. *See also* 38 C.F.R. § 7.7.
[104] 50 U.S.C. app. § 547(b)(2).
[105] *Id.* app. § 547(b)(3).
[106] *Id.* app. § 545(a). In fact, "[w]hile a policy is protected . . ., cash value, loan value, withdrawal of dividend accumulation, unearned premiums, or other value of similar character may not be available to the insured with the approval of the Secretary." *Id.* app. § 536(b). On the other hand, "[t]he right of the insured to change a beneficiary designation or select an optional settlement for a beneficiary shall not be affected." *Id.*
[107] *Id.* app. 545(a).
[108] *Id.* app. § 531. For a further discussion of the major Title III protections, *see infra* Ch. 4.
[109] 50 U.S.C. app. § 536.
[110] *Id.* app. § 536(a).
[111] *Id.* app. § 536(b).
[112] *Id.* app. § 536(d).

The court should refuse the request, however, if there is a showing that the military service materially affects "the ability of the servicemember to comply with the terms of the obligation."[113] Additionally, if the insurance policy premiums are guaranteed under the guarantee provisions,[114] they "shall not be considered due and unpaid."[115]

B. Health Insurance

Servicemembers are entitled to have their civilian health insurance reinstated when they return to civilian life following periods of active duty.[116] Additionally, the reinstatement is to be without a waiting period and there can be no exclusion for a "condition [which] arose before or during the period of . . . service"[117] as long as the condition would not have entailed an exclusion or waiting period had the servicemember remained covered[118] and "if . . . the condition has not been determined by the Secretary of Veterans Affairs to be a disability incurred or aggravated in the line of duty."[119] The servicemember must apply for reinstatement "not later than 120 days after the date of the termination or release from military service."[120]

This protection is very similar to the protections found under the Uniformed Services Employment and Reemployment Rights Act (USERRA).[121] In fact, USERRA is the governing provision[122] for servicemembers participating in employer-offered health plans.[123]

C. Professional Liability Protection

This protection was added to the SSCRA in 1991.[124] As enacted, it gave protection only to health care providers. Although the Secretary of Defense was allowed to declare other professions eligible, he did not do so until the Kosovo operations when attorneys were included.[125] Today, the SCRA expressly and permanently extends the protection to attorneys.[126]

[113] *Id.* app. § 536(c)(a).
[114] *Id.* app. §§ 541-5489.
[115] *Id.* app. § 536(d).
[116] *Id.* app. § 594(a).
[117] *Id.* app. § 594(b)(1).
[118] *Id.* app. § 594(b)(2).
[119] *Id.* app. § 594(b)(3).
[120] *Id.* app. § 594(d).
[121] 38 U.S.C. §§ 4301-4333 (2000).
[122] *Id.* § 4317.
[123] 50 U.S.C. app. § 594(c).
[124] *See* Major James Pottorff, *The Soldiers' and Sailors' Civil Relief Act Amendments of 1991*, ARMY LAW., May 1991, at 47.
[125] *See* Lieutenant Colonel Paul Conrad, *Professional Liability Protection for Attorneys Ordered to active Duty*, ARMY LAW., Aug. 1999, at 44.
[126] 50 U.S.C. app. § 593(a)(2)(A).

The Act provides that professional liability insurance can be suspended during a period of active military service.[127] The professional is to be reinstated under the coverage following release from active duty[128] without any premium increase.[129] Additionally, servicemembers are to receive refunds for premiums paid during any period of suspension[130] and actions for damages for acts prior to the period of suspension may be stayed.[131] Insurance carriers are not liable for claims during the period of suspension.[132]

Despite these protections, attorneys and other professionals should consider whether to obtain a so called "tail policy." Under most insurance contracts, practitioners may be covered at the time a claim is filed even though they were covered at the time an alleged act of professional dereliction occurs.[133]

XI. *Public Lands*

Perhaps the most obscure SCRA provisions relate to public lands. These provisions,[134] in essence, provide the servicemember who is a homestead or desert-land entryman,[135] who has a mining claim, or whose widow has a claim to such land, with the right to obtain waiver of certain requirements as to occupancy and improvement of public lands. For example, "[a] person holding a permit or lease on the public domain under the federal mineral leasing laws who enters military service may suspend all operations under the permit or lease for the duration of the military service and for 180 days thereafter.[136]

[127] *Id.* app. § 593(b)(2).
[128] *Id.* app. § 593(c).
[129] *Id.* app. § 593(d).
[130] *Id.* app. § 593(b)(2)(B).
[131] *Id.* app. § 593(f).
[132] *Id.* app. § 593(b)(3).
[133] *See, e.g.*, Patrice Wade DiPietro, *CAT [Medical Professional Liability Catastrophic Loss] Fund Not Required to Cover Default Judgment*, 7 Lawyers J. 2, 12 (2005) (medical malpractice claim discussion). The SCRA contains a provision clarifying that nonfeasance related to a failure to provide for a client's continued service are deemed to have occurred when the professional fails to provide for that continued assistance rather than when the client discovers the problem. They are deemed to have occurred during the period of coverage, but not during the period of suspension. *See* 50 U.S.C. app. § 593(b)(4). It would seem however, that this would not obviate the need for a tail policy.
[134] 50 U.S.C. app. §§ 562-569.
[135] An entryman is one who makes an entry onto homestead or desert-land as an initial step to acquiring ownership under the public land laws of the United States. Indian Cove Irr. Dist. v. Prideaux, 136 P. 618, 620 (1913).
[136] 50 U.S.C. app. § 565(a).

Chapter 3

Procedural Protections

I. *Purpose and Scope*

As noted,[1] the SCRA is divided into seven titles. Title II is called "General Relief." It may be broken down into procedural and substantive protections or benefits. This chapter will consider the SCRA's procedural protections as follows: the protection against default judgments, stays of civil and administrative proceedings, stays of judgments, and the tolling of civil statutes of limitations. The substantive Title II benefits capping interest on pre-service obligations[2] and other contractual protections are examined in Chapter 6.

II. *Default Judgment Protection*

The SCRA's default provision is markedly different from the prior legislation. Congress enhanced its explanation of the protection. In any event, it is examining out the statute in its entirety:

50 U.S.C. app. § 521

(a) Applicability of section. This section applies to any civil action or proceeding in which the defendant does not make an appearance.

(b) Affidavit requirement.

  (1) Plaintiff to file affidavit. In any action or proceeding covered by this section, the court, before entering judgment for the plaintiff, shall require the plaintiff to file with the court an affidavit——

    (A) stating whether or not the defendant is in military service and showing necessary facts to support the affidavit; or

    (B) if the plaintiff is unable to determine whether or not the defendant is in military service, stating that the plaintiff is unable to determine whether or not the defendant is in military service.

[1] *See supra* para. 1-5.

[2] *See* 50 U.S.C.S. app. § 527 (LEXIS 2006). *Chapter 3—General Relief: Procedural Protections* 3-2

(2) Appointment of attorney to represent defendant in military service. If in an action covered by this section it appears that the defendant is in military service, the court may not enter a judgment until after the court appoints an attorney to represent the defendant. If an attorney appointed under this section to represent a servicemember cannot locate the servicemember, actions by the attorney in the case shall not waive any defense of the servicemember or otherwise bind the servicemember.

(3) Defendant's military status not ascertained by affidavit. If based upon the affidavits filed in such an action, the court is unable to determine whether the defendant is in military service, the court, before entering judgment, may require the plaintiff to file a bond in an amount approved by the court. If the defendant is later found to be in military service, the bond shall be available to indemnify the defendant against any loss or damage the defendant may suffer by reason of any judgment for the plaintiff against the defendant, should the judgment be set aside in whole or in part. The bond shall remain in effect until expiration of the time for appeal and setting aside of a judgment under applicable Federal or State law or regulation or under any applicable ordinance of a political subdivision of a State. The court may issue such orders or enter such judgments as the court determines necessary to protect the rights of the defendant under this Act.

(4) Satisfaction of requirement for affidavit. The requirement for an affidavit under paragraph (1) may be satisfied by a statement, declaration, verification, or certificate, in writing, subscribed and certified or declared to be true under penalty of perjury.

(c) Penalty for making or using false affidavit. A person who makes or uses an affidavit permitted under subsection (b) (or a statement, declaration, verification, or certificate as authorized under subsection (b)(4)) knowing it to be false, shall be fined as provided in title 18, United States Code, or imprisoned for not more than one year, or both.

(d) Stay of proceedings. In an action covered by this section in which the defendant is in military service, the court shall grant a stay of proceedings for a minimum period of 90 days under this subsection upon application of counsel, or on the court's own motion, if the court determines that—

(1) there may be a defense to the action and a defense cannot be presented without the presence of the defendant; or

(2) after due diligence, counsel has been unable to contact the defendant or otherwise determine if a meritorious defense exists.

(e) Inapplicability of section 202 procedures. A stay of proceedings under subsection (d) shall not be controlled by procedures or requirements under section 202 [50 U.S.C. app. § 522].

(f) Section 202 protection. If a servicemember who is a defendant in an action covered by this section receives actual notice of the action, the servicemember may request a stay of proceeding under section 202 [50 U.S.C. app. 522].

(g) Vacation or setting aside of default judgments.

(1) Authority for court to vacate or set aside judgment. If a default judgment is entered in an action covered by this section against a servicemember during the servicemember's period of military service (or within 60 days after termination of or release from such military service), the court entering the judgment shall, upon application by or on behalf of the servicemember, reopen the judgment for the purpose of allowing the servicemember to defend the action if it appears that——

(A) the servicemember was materially affected by reason of that military service in making a defense to the action; and

(B) the servicemember has a meritorious or legal defense to the action or some part of it.

(2) Time for filing application. An application under this subsection must be filed not later than 90 days after the date of the termination of or release from military service.

(h) Protection of bona fide purchaser. If a court vacates, sets aside, or reverses a default judgment against a servicemember and the vacating, setting aside, or reversing is because of a provision of this Act that action shall not impair a right or title acquired by a bona fide purchaser for value under the default judgment.[3]

III. *Reopening Default Judgments*

The requirements of the statute are triggered when a plaintiff moves for a default judgment. That being said, it is easier to understand the statutory requirements by beginning the examination from the tail end of the procedure. In other words, by examining how a servicemember reopens a default judgment. First, the defendant-servicemember must apply to the same court that rendered the original default judgment.[4] Since default judgments obtained in violation of the SCRA are merely voidable and not void,[5] "a judgment remain[s] valid until properly attacked by a service man."[6] Next, the default judgment must have been rendered against the defendant

[3] *Id.* app. § 521.

[4] Davidson v. GFC, 295 F. Supp. 878 (N.D. Ga. 1968) (no basis for collateral attack and no federal question presented). *See supra* para. 2-6 nn. 57-60 and accompanying text.

[5] *See, e.g.*, United States v. Hampshire, 892 F. Supp. 1327 (D.Ks. 1995), *aff'd* 95 F.3d 999 (10th Cir. 1996); Krumme v. Krumme, 636 P.2d 814, 817 (1981). A void judgment would not necessitate SCRA analysis. For example, if a plaintiff took a default judgment absent service of process, then the judgment would be void. Saborit v. Wlech, 113 S.E.2d 921, 922 (1963).

[6] Ostrowski v. Pethick, 590 A.2d 1290, 1293 (1991). *See also* Collins v. Collins, 805 N.E.2d 410, 414 (Ind. Ct. App. 2004); *In re* the Paternity of T.M.Y. Kevin Nickels v. York, 725 N.E.2d, 997, 1004 (Ind. Ct. App. 2000).

servicemember during his/her period of active duty service[7] or within sixty days thereafter.[8] This excludes judgments rendered before the defendant entered military service or more than sixty days after separation from service. Additionally, the servicemember has ninety days from the end of the active service to file an application to reopen the default judgment.[9] Defendants discovering default judgments more than ninety days after termination of their military service are too late to invoke the SCRA.[10]

There are, however, three main criteria that must be met if a servicemember is to reopen a default judgment. The servicemember must not have made an appearance in the case.[11] The servicemember's military service must be shown to have materially affected his or her ability to defend the suit[12] and "the servicemember [must have] a meritorious or legal defense to the action or some part of it."[13]

A. *Defendant Must Not Have Appeared in the Case*

The SCRA states that the default protection "applies to any civil action or proceeding in which the defendant does not make an appearance."[14] The question then becomes one of what constitutes an appearance. Under the former law, the statute spoke of "a default of any appearance"[15] and tended to mean any appearance whatsoever.

> Consideration of the meaning of the phrase "any appearance" is sometimes required. The 1918 Act used the words "an appearance" but in the 1940 Act the phrase was broadened to read "any appearance." The word "appearance" is defined in Webster's New Int. Dict. 2d Ed., 1940, as meaning in law, "the coming into court of a party summoned in an action either by himself or by his attorney." Technically there are several different kinds and methods of appearance. See Am Jur, appearances, section 1, etc. A default of any appearance by the defendant means a default in any one of several ways of making an appearance. "Any" applies to every individual part without distinction.[16]

[7] The SCRA definition of active duty comes from Title 10: "The term 'active duty' means full-time duty in the active military service of the United States. Such term includes full-time training duty, annual training duty, and attendance, while in the active military service, at a school designated as a service school by law or by the Secretary of the military department concerned. Such term does not include full-time National Guard duty." 10 U.S.C. § 101(d)(1) (2000). *See also supra* para. 2-2.

[8] 50 U.S.C. app. § 521(g)(1).

[9] *Id.* app. § 521(g)(2).

[10] *See, e.g.*, Morris Plan Bank v. Hadsall, 202 Ga. 52, 53, 41 S.E.2d 881, 882 (1947) (untimely); *Collins*, 805 N.E.2d at 414 (untimely); *Nickels*, 805 N.E.2d at 1004(untimely); Smith v. Davis, 364 S.E.2d 156, 158 (1998) (timely); Radich v. Bloomberg, 54 A.2d 247, *cert. denied*, 332 U.S. 810 (1947)(

[11] 50 U.S.C. app. § 521(a).

[12] *Id.* app. § 521(g)(1).

[13] *Id.* app. § 521(g)(2).

[14] *Id.* app. § 521(a).

[15] *Id.* app. § 520(1) (2000).

[16] *In re* Cool's Estate, 18 A.2d at 716-17.

Any act before the court by a defendant-servicemember, or the defendant's attorney, will constitute an appearance depriving the servicemember of the default protections. In fact, this can even include a request for a stay pursuant to the SCRA's stay provision.[17] In *Blankenship v. Blankenship*,[18] for instance, the defendant's counsel filed an affidavit asking the court to quash the complaint and the service or continue the cause under the SSCRA's stay provisions. Following the court's entry of judgment, the defendant servicemember filed for a rehearing.[19] Although he had been in Japan during the suit, the court denied a rehearing indicating that the motion to quash or continue constituted an appearance.[20] The court did not accept the argument that there was a worthy distinction between whether the appearance was "special" or "general" because the statute looked to cover "*any*" appearance.[21] As another example, the court in *Skates v. Stockton*,[22] held that a letter to the trial court from a legal assistance attorney requesting a stay "constituted a general appearance whereby the appellant submitted to personal jurisdiction"[23] and thereby waived the servicemember's protections from suffering a default judgment.

Other courts, under similar facts, have ruled differently. In *O'Neill v. O'Neill*, the respondent servicemember's counsel filed motions to dismiss, under the state law, for lack of jurisdiction.[24] After those motions were denied, counsel sought a continuance under the SSCRA.[25] As one might guess, the respondent did not show for the trial. Despite these rather substantial efforts on the part of counsel, the Mississippi Supreme Court "[held] that [the servicemember's] motion for relief amounts to no more than an application to stay the proceedings and should not be construed as an appearance."[26] Similarly, a trial court had this to say about a letter from a legal

[17] *See* 50 U.S.C. app. § 522. *See infra* para. 3-5 (providing a discussion of this protection). In fact, the modern version of the law indicates that resort to the stay protections precludes later resort to the default provisions. *See* 50 U.S.C. app. § 522(e)("A servicemember who applies for a stay . . . and is unsuccessful may not seek the protections afforded by [50 U.S.C. app. § 521]").

[18] 82 So. 2d 335, 336 (1955).

[19] *Id.* 82 So.2d at 338-9.

[20] *Id.* at 340.

[21] *Id.* On this issue about what constitutes an appearance, *see also* Major Garth K. Chandler, *The Impact of a Request for a Stay of Proceedings Under the Soldiers' and Sailors' Civil Relief Act*, 132 MIL. L. REV. 169, 171-4 (1983).

[22] 683 P.2d 304 (1984).

[23] *Id.* at 306. *See also* Marriage of Lopez, 173 Cal. Rptr. 718, 721 (Cal. App. 1981) (letter to opposing counsel did not substitute for an actual appearance); Reynolds v. Reynolds, 134 P.2d 251 (1943) (attorneys entered appearance to contest jurisdiction);Artis-Wergin v. Artis-Wergin, N.W.2d 750 (Wis. Ct. App. 1989) (letter from legal assistance attorney).

[24] 515 So.2d 1208, 1210 (Miss. 1987).

[25] *Id.*

[26] *Id.* at 1212. *See also* Kramer v. Kramer, 668 S.W.2d 457 (Tex. Ct. App. 1984) (jurisdiction faulty for lack of minimal contacts, but servicemember's letter to court invoking SSCRA rights likewise did not constitute an appearance); Rutherford v. Bentz, 104 N.E.2d 343 (1952) (telegram to court did not amount to appearance); Vara v. Vara, 171 N.E.2d 384 (Com. Pleas Ct. 1961).

assistance attorney to a clerk of court and opposing counsel explaining that the servicemember's ability to meet certain mortgage obligations had been prejudiced by the servicemember's military service:

> [H]is "legal" advisor was the legal assistance officer—a first lieutenant in the Air Corps—stationed at a camp in a distant State. Surely, it cannot be said that this defendant is represented by authorized counsel who could, if necessary, assert on his behalf the relief which might be obtained under the Federal or State Soldiers' and Sailors' Civil Relief Act.[27]

The requirement for the court to appoint an attorney to represent a defaulting defendant-servicemember is discussed later in this chapter, but it should be noted at this point that the actions of the court-appointed attorney will not generally bind the servicemember.[28]

The new legislation respecting the right or opportunity for a servicemember to stay civil proceedings must be kept in mind. A request for a stay may amount to the entry of appearance, but the servicemember still has other options. In other words, while an appearance will preclude resort to the default protections, the picture is not completely bleak.[29]

B. The Servicemembers' Military Service Must Have Materially Affected Ability to Defend

The next significant criterion is that the servicemember's military duties materially affect, that is prejudice, his/her ability to defend the suit at the time the default judgment is entered.[30]

On this question of fact, the trial courts are given wide discretion.[31] Servicemembers must show that at the time of judgment they were prejudiced in their ability to defend the suit because of their service. The courts have ruled that a voidable default judgment is subject to being vacated at the instance of a servicemember, but only upon proper showing that the servicemember's defense has been prejudiced by reason of

[27] Bowery Savings Bank v. Pellegrino, 185 Misc. 912, 914, 58 N.Y.S.2d 771, 773 (Sup. Ct. 1945). The facts in the case are not fully explained, but it seems apparent that the servicemember had hoped to avail himself of the former law's mortgage protection provisions. For the current provision, *see* 50 U.S.C. app. § 533 (LEXIS 2006).

[28] 50 U.S.C. app. § 521(b)(2). *See also infra* para. 3-4b.

[29] *See generally* 50 U.S.C. app. § 521. *See also infra* para. 3-6.

[30] 50 U.S.C. app. § 521(g)(1).

[31] LaMar v. LaMar, 505 P.2d 566, 568 (1973); Krumme v. Krumme, 636 P.2d 814, 817 (1981); Ostrowski v. Pethick, 590 A.2d 1290, 1293 (1991)

military service.[32] In *Becknell v. D'Angelo*,[33] the court vacated an amended divorce decree of a servicemember who had left the continental United States before a hearing on his wife's motion to amend, even though he had appeared at the hearing on the initial decree. His military service prejudiced his ability to defend in the action.[34] In *Federal Home Loan Mortgage Corp. v. Taylor*,[35] the court held the acceleration of the entire mortgage debt due to default on one month's installment was unconscionable. Gaps in payments were attributable, in large part, to the mortgagor husband's military service in the Philippines.[36] In *Hawkins v. Hawkins*, [37] a case involving paternity, child support, and the division of retirement pay, the court found ample prejudice where the servicemember was unable to take leave to defend the action.[38] In fact, the court remarked that "the inability to obtain leave from military service in order to conduct a proper defense is exactly the type of situation the act was created to address."[39] Finally, in cases where the servicemember is stationed overseas, it is possible for a court to find that the overseas service amounts to a prima facie showing of prejudice; that is, a finding that the military service has materially affected the servicemember's ability to defend the suit.[40]

[32] *See, e.g.*, Allen v. Allen, 182 P.2d 551, 553 (1947) (servicemember "unquestionably prejudiced by reason of his military service in making his defense"); Unsatisfied Claim & Judgment Fund Board v. Fortney, 285 A.2d 641, 645 (1971) ("an opportunity should be afforded to the defendant upon the remand to show whether he was prejudiced by reason of his military service and whether he in fact has a meritorious or legal defense to the action"); Smith v. Davis, 364 S.E.2d 156, 158 (1988) (prejudice found where servicemember "stationed in California assigned to a unit that at anytime could be sent to the western Pacific"); Cornell Leasing Corp. v. Hemmingway, 553 N.Y.S.2d 285 (N.Y. Civ. Ct. 1990) (no showing of prejudice where servicemember lived in vicinity of court and status as reserve or active soldier was unclear); Thompson v. Lowman, 155 N.E.2d 258, *aff'g* 155 N.E.2d 250 (1958).

[33] 506 S.W.2d 688 (Tex. Civ. App. 1974).

[34] *Id.*at 693.

[35] 318 So. 2d 203 (Fla. App. 1975).

[36] *Id.* The result may also have been attributable to the fact that the servicemember's child was sent back to a hospital in Texas. This necessitated that the servicemember's spouse reside in an apartment near the child's location. While the child's condition may not have had anything to do with the military service, the necessity of having to send her to a distant facility was because of the military service. *Id.* at 207.

[37] Hawkins v. Hawkins, 999 S.W.2d 171 (Tex. App. 1999).

[38] *Id.* at 175.

[39] *Id.*

[40] *See e.g.*, Saborit v. Welch, 133 S.E.2d 921 (1963); Murdock v. Murdock, 526 S.E.2d 241, 246 (S.C. App. 1999) ("For the clerk or the judge to fail to acknowledge that the husband was in the military and his reason for not appearing was because he was stationed in Japan is disconcerting"). *But see* LaMar v. LaMar, 505 P.2d 566 (1973) (no abuse of discretion to refuse to vacate default divorce judgment obtained against servicemember stationed abroad, where he was fully informed of action, took no steps to protect any rights he might have cared to assert, and made no attempt to stay proceedings).

As much as deployments, leave policies, and overseas assignments can clearly impact a servicemember, the opposite can also be true. In the bulk of litigation it is doubtful that military service creates any more of an impact than any other pursuit. How difficult is it, in most cases, for a servicemember to defend a suit in a state court near the installation? Like any other citizen, the servicemember may have to work through an attorney to schedule convenient dates, but the military service will not have an adverse impact. [41] In sum, "[a] soldier . . . is not entitled to relief under the Soldiers' and Sailors' Civil Relief Act as a consequence of his membership in the armed services but, rather, because his defense is materially affected by his military service."[42] Further, the burden of proof is on the servicemember to prove this point.[43]

C. Servicemember Must Have a Meritorious Defense

Closely linked to the requirement that the servicemember's service must materially affect or prejudice his/her ability to defend the suit, is the requirement that the servicemember have a meritorious defense to the suit.[44] That is, at the time of the default judgment, the servicemember could not defend the suit because of military service, but if s/he had been able to, s/he would have been able to offer up a defense.

This is not to say that the servicemember must have a defense that would have prevailed. It is merely that the servicemember would have offered a cogent defense to the trier of fact had the matter actually gone to trial. In other words, "in a hearing under this section . . . the court does not decide the issue . . . it decide[s] only if there [is] an issue between the parties which would entitle the defendant to a trial."[45] To ultimately succeed on the merits, however, the service member must still have a meritorious defense.

Although the servicemember would not have to prove the case when moving to set aside the default judgment, "facts showing a meritorious defense should be pleaded."[46] In more concrete terms, a defendant might assert that he was not the father

[41] Burgess v. Burgess, 234 N.Y.S.2d 87 (1962). In *Burgess*, the servicemember was stationed where "he was always accessible to the court" and he had been "fully informed of the pendency of the action." *Id.* at 89. Additionally, the day before the inquest, which ultimately resulted in a default judgment, the servicemember's attorney had called for the servicemember only to find that he was on leave. One can infer that it was his leave, rather than any requirement of the military, that prevented his attendance. *Id.*

[42] Wilson v. Butler, 584 So.2d 414, 416 (Miss. 1991) (citing Roberts v. Fuhr, 523 So.2d 20, 28 (Miss. 1987). Ironically, the defendant-soldier in *Wilson* was stationed at Fort Ord, California. Thus, there may have been evidence that would have supported a claim of material effect. The point, however, is that he did not present evidence to prove the point. *Id.*

[43] *Id.*

[44] 50 U.S.C.S. app. § 521(g)(1)(B) (LEXIS 2006).

[45] Kirby v. Holman, 25 N.W.2d 664, 675 (1947). In construing a similar Iowa rule, the court also stated that "[t]he requirement that the petition allege a meritorious defense does not require the allegation of a defense which can be guaranteed to prevail at a trial and there need be no evidence to establish the defense." *Id.* at 675.

[46] Thompson v. Lowman, 155 N.E.2d 258, 261 (1958).

in a paternity case[47] or that he was not receiving pay in a child support matter.[48] The servicemember might plead that he has "tender[ed] payment prior to foreclosure,"[49] but the servicemember will have to make more than a mere argument or claim to a meritorious defense.[50]

D. Protection of Bona Fide Purchaser

In the event a court sets aside a default judgment taken against a servicemember who is able to show prejudice and a meritorious defense, "that action shall not impair a right or title acquired by a bona fide purchaser for value under the default judgment."[51]

IV. Moving for a Default Judgment

Having considered the protection available when a servicemember seeks to set aside a default judgment, it must be noted that there are other requirements that must be followed at the time a party moves for default on the case or for default with respect to a particular aspect of the litigation. This section will outline those requirements and highlight their upshots.

First, the moving party must file an affidavit.[52] The affidavit must indicate whether the defendant is in the military service, not in the military service or whether the defendant's status cannot be determined. If the servicemember is absent, then the court must look to appoint an attorney for the absent servicemember.[53] Much litigation has revolved around affidavits indicating that the defendant is not in the military service, false affidavits, and the lack of an affidavit. These scenarios, along with the requirements for when the defendant's status is unknown, are discussed in Subsection a, below. The requirements and issues surrounding a defendant who is in the military service are taken up in Subsection b, below.

A. Affidavit

The Act provides that before judgment in any action in any court, if there is a default of any appearance by the defendant, the plaintiff must file an affidavit stating facts showing whether the defendant is in military service.

[47] *See, e.g.*, Hawkins v. Hawkins, 999 S.W.2d 171, 176 (Tex. App. 1999) (mother of child, in answers to interrogatories, admitted to having sexual relations with other men and servicemember was outside state at probable time of conception).

[48] *See, e.g.*, Smith v. Davis, 364 S.E.2d 156 (1988).

[49] Flagg v. Sun Inv. & Loan Corp., 373 P.2d 226, 229 (Okla. 1962).

[50] Urbana College v. Conway, 502 N.E.2d 675, 678 (1985) ("allegations describe a counterclaim, rather than a defense"). *See also*; LaMar v. LaMar, 505 P.2d 566 (Ariz. App. 1973) ("motion to vacate must not only declare that movant has a good and meritorious defense to the action but must also set out what it is"); Martin v. Martin, 292 S.W.2d 9 (1956) (failure to show a meritorious defense).

[51] 50 U.S.C.S. app. § 521(h) (LEXIS 2006).

[52] *Id.* app. § 521(b)(1).

[53] *Id.* app. § 521(b)(2).

1. When Required

The Act is clear that this subsection applies to any civil action or proceeding in any court. There has been little controversy on this point, although courts have ruled that presentation of a will for probate was not an adversary proceeding and interested parties need not appear before the court. Therefore, the court did not require an affidavit by the plaintiff (petitioner) when the minor son of the deceased was in military service.[54] The court held that the former SSCRA applied only when servicemembers are sued as defendants. It did not apply to *in rem* and similar proceedings that were not against named defendants.[55] Nevertheless, the majority of decisions have included probate cases within the scope of this subsection.[56]

More precisely, the requirement for the plaintiff to file an affidavit kicks in when "the defendant does not make an appearance."[57] Courts have been known, however, to make a distinction between a preliminary declaration or notation of default and a judgment of default with the affidavit not being required until the court reaches the latter step.[58]

2. Content

Again, there are three "choices" a plaintiff/moving party may make when filling out the affidavit: that the defendant is in the military service, that the defendant is not in the military service, or that the plaintiff does not know whether the defendant is in the military service.[59] If the affidavit alleges that the defendant is or is not in the military service, then it must go on and bring out "facts to support the affidavit."[60] There must

[54]Case v. Case, 124 N.E.2d 856 (Ohio Probate Ct. 1955). *See also* McLaughlin v. McLaughlin, 46 A.2d 307 (1946). *But see* Lavender v. Gernhart, 92 A.2d 751 (1952) (indicates that "probate of a will in common form is not a judgment, action or proceeding," but a caveat, or issue concerning a will's validity is another matter and something to which the SCRA will apply).

[55] *Case*, 124 N.E.2d at 859.

[56] *See, e.g.*, *In re* Ehlke's Estate, 27 N.W.2d 754 (1947); *In re* Cool's Estate, 18 A.2d 714 (1941); *In re* Larson, 183 P.2d 688 (1947) (action to change child's surname), *overruled on other grounds by* Schiffman v. Schiffman, 620 P.2d 579 (1980); Steingrabe Estate, 1 Pa. D. & C.3d 164 (1976). *See also* State *ex rel.* Estate of Perry v. Roper, 168 S.W..3d 577 (Mo. Ct. App. 2005).

[57] 50 U.S.C. app. § 521(a).

[58] *See, e.g.*, Interinsurance Exchange of the Automobile Club of S. California v. Collins, 37 Cal. Rptr. 2d 126 (1994).

[59] 50 U.S.C. app. § 521(b)(1).

[60] *Id.* app. § 521(b)(1)(A).

be, that is, some explanation for how the affiant came to the conclusion.[61] To accomplish this, the plaintiff should consider the inquiry to be in the nature of "an investigation."[62]

Some trial courts have been quite clear about what they feel is acceptable. Consider the following description from a case involving "commercial nonpayment" and a number of respondents: [63]

> In the case at bar, petitioner's agent avers that on Tuesday, April 9, 2002, at 9:20 A.M., Wednesday, April 10, 2002, at about 1:00 P.M., and Thursday, April 11, 2002, at 4:35 P.M., he went to the premises at issue to inquire whether respondent was in the military or dependent on someone in the military, but the store was consistently closed. . . . He further avers that in January 2002, when respondent applied to lease the premises as a cellular phone store, he told the agent he was self—employed, and did not state that he was in the military or dependent on someone in the military. The agent never saw respondent in a military uniform . . . The affidavit does not state, however, whether respondent completed a written application which might contain more information such as his age, references, home address, banking references, alternative telephone numbers, or other means by which respondent might be reached. Indeed, there is no indication whether the written lease for this premises, as is often true in commercial cases, provides a secondary address for the respondent for the service of notices. Finally, the court notes that it is possible to obtain an individual's military status by contacting the military service directly. This apparently was not done.[64]

The court did not find these efforts sufficient.[65] It did grant the plaintiff an opportunity to revisit the matter with the filing of a new affidavit[66] and it gave the plaintiff guidance about what it expected to find in the subsequent affidavit:

> Proof of further investigation, including at least another visit to the premises during the business hours posted on the storefront, if any, or during customary business hours if no such hours are posted. In addition the movant shall annex

[61] *See* Toyota Motor Credit Corp. v. Montano (*In re* Montano), 192 B.R. 843,846 (D. Md. 1996) ("fail[ure] to reflect any facts underlying the declaration or any investigation undertaken before filing the statement"); United States v. Simmons, 508 F. Supp. 552 (E.D. Tenn. 1980) (affidavit in question "contains not the slightest hint as to . . . what fact(s) the affiant's stated . . . 'best information and belief' . . . were acquired"). *See also* Heritage East-West, LLC. v. Fairlough Kennedy Plaza, LLC., 785 N.Y.S.2d 317, 322 (N.Y. City Civ. Ct. 2004) (court became suspicious of affidavit where affiant "attested that she spoke to two persons at the *same time* on the *same date* and in some instances . . . to the same person at the same time about several Respondents"); Mill Rock Plaza Associates v. Lively, 580 N.Y.S.2d 815 (N.Y. City Civ. Ct. 1990).

[62] Citibank, N.A. v. McGarvey, 765 N.Y.S.2d 163, 168 (N.Y. City Civ. Ct. 2003).

[63] 21948, LLC v. Mohammand Riaz, 745 N.Y.S.2d 389, 390 (N.Y. City Civ. Ct. 2002).

[64] *Id.* at 390-1.

[65] *Id.* at 391.

> a copy of any written lease or rental application, as well as an affidavit explaining what efforts it has undertaken to ascertain respondent's military status from the military. It is therefore ordered that petitioner's motion to dispense with the affidavit of nonmilitary service is denied without prejudice to renew upon submission of proof of further investigation as to the status of the respondent.[67]

Courts have been known to read the affidavits very closely. In one case, the affiant indicated that he had spoken with the defendant. The defendant denied being in the military service and was wearing civilian clothes at the time.[68] While one might consider that good enough, the court focused on the fact that the statement was good at the time when the defendant was served and not, as the statute required, "before entering judgment."[69]

As to the technical aspects of the affidavit, the SCRA indicates that the requirement "may be satisfied by a statement, declaration, verification, or certificate in writing, subscribed and certified or declared to be true under penalty of perjury."[70] Amazingly, even these simple requirements have been subject to litigation. An Idaho court, looking at the former provision, held that a verified complaint containing statements as to the defendant's military status complied with the statutory requirement for an affidavit because allegation of non-military service was made under oath.[71]

3. Persons Protected

Occasionally, a civilian defendant will assert that the plaintiff failed to file an affidavit as to the defendant's military status. The argument of course being that the defendant's rights have been violated and the default judgment should be vacated. In this situation, a Michigan court pointed out that plaintiff's failure to file an affidavit of nonmilitary service before taking default judgment did not prejudice defendants who were admittedly not in military service at the time the default was entered.[72] In a more recent case, it was noted that "[i]f . . . a clerk enters a default judgment on the basis of a defective nonmilitary affidavit, vacature under the [SSCRA] may be had only upon a showing that the defendant was a member of the class to be protected by the act and had a meritorious defense to the claim."[73] As a consequence "[a]bsent such a showing, no

[66] *Id.*

[67] *Id.* For a similar discussion *see* Benabi Realty Mgmt. Co., LLC v. Doorne, 738 N.Y.S.2d 166 (N.Y. City Civ. Ct. 2001). *See also* Hart, Nininger, & Campbell Assocs., Inc. v. Rogers, 548 A.2d 758, 769 (1988) (plaintiff's proof on nonmilitary status of defendant sufficient).

[68] Nat'l Bank of Far Rockaway v. Van Tassell, 36 N.Y.S.2d 478, 479-80 (N.Y. Sup. Ct. 1942).

[69] *Id.* at 480.

[70] 50 U.S.C.S. app. § 521(b)(4) (LEXIS 2006).

[71] Bedwell v. Bedwell, 195 P.2d 1001 (1948).

[72] Haller v. Walczak, 79 N.W.2d 622 (1956).

[73] Citibank, N.A. v. McGarvey, 765 N.Y.S.2d 163, 170 (N.Y. City Civ. Ct. 2003).

[74] *Id.*

matter how irregular the nonmilitary affidavit, the act simply does not afford an independent ground upon which a default judgment can be voided automatically."[74] In any event, the courts have agreed that the affidavit requirement protects only the military defendant who cannot appear in defense.[75] Logical though this outcome may be, it does not obviate the need to ascertain the status of the defendant.

4. Failure to File Affidavit

There is an argument that the courts are split over the effect of a plaintiff's failure to file the requisite affidavit. Some courts describe the requirement as "mandatory,"[76] and others consider that they must provide a "super-scrupulous review."[77] On the other hand, some courts "disagree" with the "mandatory" characterization,[78] while other courts note that the affidavit must be specific about the person's status at the time of the default judgment,[79] and that the declaration of default is distinct from the judgment itself.[80] The logic and analysis, however, run a bit deeper as the courts should ultimately recognize that the failure to file an affidavit when the person is in the military service does have consequences:

> It will be observed that the filing of the military affidavit is not made a jurisdictional matter. The Act authorizes entry of judgment notwithstanding the absence of the affidavit when an order of court directing such entry has been secured. The failure to file such affidavit does not affect the judgment, and is only an irregularity. . . .
>
> When the judgment is rendered without filing the requisite affidavit, the courts have uniformly ruled that the judgment is not void, but only voidable, subject to being vacated at the instance of the service member, but only upon proper showing that he has been prejudiced by reason of his military service in making defense.[81]

[75] *See, e.g.*, Tabas v. Robert Dev. Co., 297 A.2d 481, 484 (1972) ("only a defendant actually in the military service of the United States may take advantage of the Plaintiff's failure to file the proper non-military affidavit since the Act and Local Rules of Court adopted to supplement it, were designed solely to protect only persons in the military service"). *See also* Franklyn v. Elliott, 188 A.2d 345 (D.C. 1963); Miller v. Werner, 185 A.2d 723 (D.C. 1962); Vision Serv. Plan of Penn. v. Penn. AFSCME Health and Welfare Fund, 474 A.2d 339 (Pa. Super. Ct. 1984); Carberry v. Fleet, 32 Pa. D & C3d 574 (1984); Poccia v. Benson, 208 A.2d 102 (1965).

[76] Murdock v. Murdock, 526 S.E.2d 241, 247 (1999).

[77] *McGarvey*, 765 N.Y.S.2d at 170.

[78] PNC Bank, N.A. v. Kemenash, 761 A.2d 118, 120 (2000).

[79] Nat'l Bank of Far Rockaway v. Van Tassell, 36 N.Y.S.2d 478, 479-80 (N.Y. Sup. Ct. 1942).

[80] Interinsurance Exchange of the Automobile Club of S. California v. Collins, 37 Cal. Rptr.2d 126 (1994).

[81] Thompson v. Lowman, 155 N.E.2d 258, 261, *aff'g*, 155 N.E.2d 250 (Ohio C.P. 1958). *Id.* at 261. In fact, notwithstanding the *Kemenash* court's terse statement, its analysis of a state law provision and the SSCRA shows that it recognizes as well the notion that the absence of an affidavit means the judgment "is not void but voidable." *Kemenash*, 761 A.2d at 121. *See also* Hawkins v. Hawkins, 999 S.W.2d 171, 174 (Tex. App. 1999); Hernandez v. King, 411 So.2d 758 (La. Ct. App. 1982).

[82] 50 U.S.C.S. app. § 521(c) (LEXIS 2006).

5. *False Affidavits*

The SCRA makes it a federal misdemeanor to file a false affidavit.[82] A case involving a process server is illustrative of how a person might come to run afoul of this sanction. In *United States v. Kaufman*,[83] Kaufman worked as a process server for an attorney who apparently did volume collection work.[84] He was found guilty of falsely swearing on ninety counts for violating the SSCRA.[85] The story of his crimes was summed up as follows:

> In these affidavits, Kaufman represented that he had personally spoken to the defaulting defendants and had determined that they were not in the military service. The appellant conceded at trial that these conversations never took place. In the course of the customary routine of the office, a fellow employee delivered the non—military affidavits, often in large batches, to Kaufman's desk for his signature; some contained the name of the subject defendant and others left a blank where the name was supposed to be. In either event Kaufman signed them all. When he finished, he returned the documents to the clerk from whom he had received them, or he took them personally to a notary public in the office. The affidavits were then stamped and signed by the notary, but, according to Kaufman and one of the office notaries who testified at the trial, no oath was ever administered even though each document concluded with the words "Sworn to before me this day . . ."[86]

Of course an attorney can be subject to disciplinary action for lack of candor before a tribunal[87] for filing a false affidavit or for "offer[ing] evidence that the lawyer knows to be false."[88] Alternatively, an attorney could be sanctioned for lack of competence for inattentiveness and neglect if the affidavit is not proper in some respect.[89] The attorney must also take care when attesting to the veracity of the client's information. As noted, there has to be an investigation into the person's status lest the court be left to ponder "why counsel expose themselves to potential problems by filing non-military affidavits where counsel's knowledge is based upon information passed on by the client."[90]

In sum, the courts will be disturbed over a false affidavit. While a false affidavit may not obviate the need to look into whether the service has caused a material effect and whether the defendant has a meritorious defense, it may seriously curtail that

[83] 453 F.2d 306 (2d Cir. 1971).

[84] *Id.* at 308.

[85] *Id.*

[86] *Id.*

[87] Model Rules of Prof. Conduct R. 3.3(a)(1) (2002).

[88] *Id.* at R. 3.3(a)(3).

[89] *Id.* at R. 1.1. *See, e.g.*, Att'y Grievance Comm'n v. Kemp, 641 A.2d 510 (1994) (attorney not sanctioned, but blank spaces on military affidavits called into question his competence).

[90] Toyota Motor Credit Corp. v. Montano (*In re* Montano), 192 B.R. 843,846 (D. Md. 1996).

[91] Kirby v. Holman, 25 N.W.2d 664, 676-7 (1947).

analysis. This is because "[i]t certainly is not within the spirit and intent of the act that they be deprived of these defenses when there is a showing that knowledge that a defendant was in service was fraudulently withheld from the court.[91]

6. Status of Servicemember Unknown

As can be seen from the foregoing, many controversies surrounding the affidavit requirement come about from affidavits which allege that the defendant is not in the military service, a failure to file an affidavit, and false affidavits. The main requirements for what to do when the defendant is serving on active duty are discussed in the subsection concerning court appointed attorneys, below. Before looking at those requirements, it is worth considering what the plaintiff and court must do when the plaintiff is unable to ascertain the defendant's status.

When it is not possible to know whether the defendant is in military service, the court "may require the plaintiff to file a bond."[92] Simply stated, if the defendant turns up and "is . . . found to be in military service, the bond shall be available to indemnify the defendant against any loss or damage the defendant may suffer by reason of any judgment for the plaintiff against the defendant."[93]

7. Timing of Motion for Default

In a traditional sense, one often thinks of default judgments being entered shortly after a defendant fails to answer or otherwise appear in a case. Things can be more complicated and a judgment tantamount to a default judgment can occur at any time. In fact, the SCRA defines judgment very broadly to include "any judgment, decree, order, or ruling, final or temporary."[94] Thus, focus needs be placed on the meaning of any court decision.

The notion that a default judgment can occur at any time during the course of litigation is most apt to be true when the litigation involves a family law matter. A marriage may be dissolved, but certain issues which were previously resolved such as visitation, debt allocation, and child support can be then subsequently revisited. When that happens, the servicemember may have participated fully in the litigation, but the nature of the service of process, their appearance and so on need to be examined on their own merits at subsequent proceedings. In *Murdock v. Murdock*,[95] the parties were divorced in 1997. The order dissolving the marriage also commanded that the parties reach an agreement as to the payment of certain debts.[96] As one might guess, they were not able to do so. Although the trial court originally continued a hearing on child support to allow the husband more time to obtain counsel, it ultimately entered a judgment against him for child support and debt allocation.[97] The appellate court found

[92] 50 U.S.C.S. app. § 521(b)(3) (LEXIS 2006).
[93] *Id.*
[94] *Id.* app. § 511(9).
[95] 526 S.E.2d 241 (S.C. App. 1999).
[96] *Id.* at 243.
[97] *Id.* at 244.
[98] *Id.* at 246.

that this judgment was in fact a default judgment and subject to scrutiny under the SSCRA.[98] The servicemember, being stationed in Japan, was materially affected by his military service.[99] His alleged payment of the child support was a meritorious defense.[100] More importantly, even though the husband had waived his rights under the SSCRA in the original action, it was held that this subsequent proceeding "was a separate action."[101]

B. Court-Appointed Attorney

As previously stated, in every civil suit where a party seeks to default the opponent, the moving party must file an affidavit indicating that the defendant is not in the active military service, that it cannot be determined whether the defendant is in the military service, or that the defendant is in the military service. Although much of the litigation discussed thus far is relevant to the latter possibility, this subsection will discuss the primary requirements that follow from a declaration by the movant that the party in default is in military service.

1. General

If the plaintiff/moving party determines that the defendant/party in default is in the military service, then "the court *may not* enter a judgment until after the court appoints an attorney to represent the defendant."[102] By adopting the SCRA provisions, Congress has meant to strengthen and clarify the law's requirements. Thus, much of the prior case law is still relevant as a guide to proper interpretation.

That being said, there has always been a number of questions about the court-appointed attorney's role. This may have been due, in part, to the fact that the prior legislation contained two provisions offering differing wording regarding the court-appointed attorney. One passage indicated that a court "may appoint" the attorney[103] and the other indicated that the court "shall" appoint.[104] In the first instance, the appointment was permissive when it was known that the party was in the military service and had not yet appeared.[105] The appointment was mandatory before entry of a default judgment where there was a default of appearance and where "an affidavit is not filed showing that the defendant is not in the military service."[106] Under these circumstances, the attorney's role was defined "to represent [the] defendant and protect his interest."[107]

[99] *Id.*
[100] *Id.* at 247.
[101] *Id.* at 247. Although the court was concerned with what it saw as a failure to apply mandatory SSCRA requirements, it also found that the failure to provide notice to the servicemember about the substance of the hearing in question violated due process standards. *Id.* at 247-8.
[102] 50 U.S.C.S. app. § 521(b)(2) (LEXIS 2006).
[103] 50 U.S.C. app. § 520(3) (2000).
[104] *Id.* app. § 520(1).
[105] *Id.* app. § 520(3).
[106] *Id.* app. § 520(1).
[107] *Id.*
[108] For a discussion of the appearance element, *see supra* para. 3-3a.

The modern provision is obviously clearer as it works to make the appointment a prerequisite to entry of the default judgment. Even so, the scope of the representation is worth considering further as well as certain other attendant issues.

2. Appearance/Prior Representation

It is axiomatic that the need to appoint an attorney does not come about if the defendant already has an attorney. Additionally, there is no need to resort to this section of the protection unless the defendant has defaulted of any appearance whatsoever.[108] For example, the California Supreme Court held that this protection was designed to protect defendants in military service who do not appear by ensuring appointment of attorneys to represent them. The section did not protect a defendant who had appointed his own attorneys to protect his interests.[109] An interesting situation can arise when a servicemember retains an attorney from previous, related litigation. In such a situation, the California court ruled that, where notice of a wife's motion to modify a support order was served upon an absent husband's attorney in the original divorce action, but the attorney stated he was no longer authorized to represent defendant and had not been able to communicate with the husband, it was error to fail to appoint an attorney.[110]

3. Functions of the Court-Appointed Attorney

The SCRA is a bit vague on the functions the court-appointed attorney is to perform. It does talk, at one point, about attempting to locate the servicemember.[111] Broadly, the attorney can be thought of and has been described as a guardian *ad litem*[112] or as an attorney *ad litem*.[113] One author has noted that an "appointed attorney is under an obligation to exhaust every reasonable means of establishing contact with the service member prior to trial date so that some logical course of action can be agreed upon."[114] In one case, the court found that the purpose of the appointed counsel is to obtain a stay for the defendant.[115] In fact, the current statute suggests that obtaining a stay is among the attorney's duties.[116]

One aspect of the "representation" which is clear concerns the non-binding nature of anything the attorney does on behalf of the servicemember. Under the prior law, it was clear that nothing a court appointed attorney did could amount to an appearance on behalf of a service member.[117] The prior legislation indicated that "no attorney

[109] Reynolds v. Reynolds, 134 P.2d 251 (1943).

[110] Allen v. Allen, 182 P.2d 551 (1947). *See also supra* para. 3-4(b)(4).

[111] 50 U.S.C.S. app. § 521(b)(2) (LEXIS 2006).

[112] *See* Rutherford v. Bentz, 104 N.E.2d 343 (1952).

[113] *In re* Ehlke's Estate, 27 N.W.2d 754 (1947).

[114] Dwan V. Kerig, *The Absent Defendant and the Federal Soldiers' and Sailors' Civil Relief Act,* 33 N.Y.U. L. REV. 975, 980 (1958).

[115] In re *Ehlke's Estate*, 27 N.W.2d at 757.

[116] *See* 50 U.S.C. app. § 521(d).

[117] *See, e.g., Rutherford*, 104 N.E.2d at 346. *See also* Kerig, *supra* note 114, at 981.

[118] 50 U.S.C. app. § 520(3)(2000). A servicemember's actions could change the course of events.

appointed under this Act to protect a person in military service shall have power to waive any right of the person for whom he is appointed or bind him by his acts."[118] Under the new legislation the provision has changed to indicated that "[i]f an attorney appointed under this section to represent a servicemember cannot locate the servicemember, actions by the attorney in the case shall not waive any defense of the servicemember or otherwise bind the servicemember."[119] Thus, even under the newer provision, the attorney's presence would not amount to an appearance on behalf of the absent servicemember. The only open question would be whether the acts of the attorney serve to bind the defendant-servicemember when the attorney is able to locate that servicemember.

Of course, once servicemembers begin authorizing acts by their appointed attorneys, they will ordinarily be bound thereby. The Supreme Court of Washington has said:

> It appears from the language of the Act that the protection afforded a service member from any waiver of his rights by legal counsel was intended to apply only where the attorney acted under authority of the court, rather than authority of the service member. In each case a question of fact exists; *i.e.*, whether service member has, himself, authorized the attorney to act for him. That the attorney was originally appointed under the act is no wise determinative of this question.[120]

It is also obvious that there are limits on what the attorney should do; that is, there are things the attorney should not do. In one case, the appointed counsel looked to examine the file, gauge whether his client's interest was at stake, and obtain "a stay to enable him to consult his client."[121] The court granted the stay but additionally it may have sent him off on a tangent when it allowed that the stay would be for "ample time to make an investigation and 'array' his witnesses and present the matter as fully as possible."[122] As one can guess, the attorney proceeded from that point to do quite a few things on his client's behalf, although he ultimately did very little in the way of communicating with his client.[123] In any event, the state supreme court characterized the

For example, as one court remarked, "[o]nce the appellant knew of the action and authorized his court-appointed attorney to appear on his behalf, the appellant was no longer entitled to further benefits under the Soldiers' and Sailors' Civil Relief Act of 1940." In the Matter of Roslyn B. v. Alfred G., 635 N.Y.S.2d 283, 284, 222 A.D.2d 581, 582 (1995).

[119] 50 U.S.C.S. app. § 521(b)(2) (LEXIS 2006).

[120] Sanders v. Sanders, 388 P.2d 942, 945 (1964). *See also* Bell v. Nugent (*In re* Nugent), 955 P.2d 584, 589 (Colo. App. 1997) ("question of fact whether a member has authorized an attorney to act").

[121] *In re* Ehlke's Estate, 27 N.W.2d 754, 755 (1947).

[122] *Id*. at 756.

[123] *Id*.

[124] *Id*.

representation as "alleged service"[124] and held that "the utmost service of a person appointed to appear for a soldier in the military service, either required or suggested, is toward procuring a temporary stay of proceedings as is necessary to protect the soldier's interest."[125]

In reality, the chores for the court-appointed attorney may be a bit broader than merely asking for a stay of the proceedings. Even if a continuance is the ultimate goal, it is hard to argue that the following guidance from a trial court to its appointed counsel is overdone:

1. contact the defendant and assure that defendant has actual notice of the lawsuit,
2. advise defendant of the protections of the Soldiers' and Sailors' Civil Relief Act,
3. advise defendant of the possibility of entry of default judgment and of the consequences of such a judgment,
4. ascertain whether defendant's ability to appear and defend his or her legal interests is affected in any way by defendant's military status, and
5. if the defendant wishes, move for a stay of the proceedings to enable defendant to obtain counsel or prepare a defense on the merits of the case.[126]

Although the appointment of an attorney in these types of matters is onerous and time-consuming, it is not something to be taken lightly. As *Kramer v. Kramer*[127] establishes, inattentive practices such as appointing the attorney "some minutes before trial was to begin"[128] are frowned upon.

4. Failure to Appoint Attorney

As with the failure to file an affidavit, the failure to appoint an attorney renders the judgment voidable, but not void. Once it is established that the court has missed this step, the inquiry will turn to whether the defendant's military service has materially affected or prejudiced his/her ability to defend the action and, if so, whether the defendant has a meritorious defense.[129]

5. Court-Appointed Attorney Compensation

The SCRA is silent concerning whether and how to pay the attorney for his/her involvement in the case. A New Jersey court, in dictum, stated:

> Ordinarily the services rendered by proctor and counsel so appointed are to be regarded as a patriotic duty for which no compensation would be expected by

[125] *Id.* at 757. *See also* Rutherford v. Bentz, 104 N.E.2d 343, 345 (1952) (improper for appointed counsel to have "examined witnesses and acted as attorney for the defendant").

[126] State of Alaska *ex rel.* Dew v. Superior Court, 907 P.2d 14, 14 n.2 (Alaska 1995).

[127] 668 S.W.2d 457 (Tex. App. 1984).

[128] *Id.* at 458.

[129] Hawkins v. Hawkins, 999 S.W.2d 171 (Tex. App. 1999);

[130] *In re* Cool's Estate, 18 A.2d 714, 717.

> members of a profession deeply imbued by a sense of public responsibility. Certainly not as against a party in military service. However, in cases in which allowances are commonly made according to the usual probate practice, there seems no good reason why reasonable compensation should not be awarded.[130]

Similarly, the Wisconsin Supreme Court held that the county court should pay the attorney, but the "compensation . . . should be measured by compensation commonly allowed to those in the public service, rather than the fees ordinarily chargeable between attorney and client."[131] Setting the fee is one thing, but determining who pays is another. As the Wisconsin court indicated, it should be the court. Others have come to the same conclusion.[132] Another court held that the plaintiffs would bear the costs.[133] If it is a probate matter, then perhaps the compensation will come from the estate.[134] In other jurisdictions, the result may depend on who prevails, but in others a local rule may be in place.[135]

V. Stays of Civil and Administrative Proceedings

A. General

One of the most significant SCRA benefits calls for stays of civil and administrative proceedings. This provision is of obvious benefit to members of the Guard and Reserves who are in the middle of litigation but called to rapidly mobilize. It is of benefit to members of the active component when they face suit while deployed or otherwise when they are a significant distance from the courtroom.[136]

The SCRA actually contains several stay provisions.[137] The main provision, broadly applicable to civil and administrative proceedings, is as follows:

> 50 U.S.C. app. § 522
>
> (a) Applicability of section. This section applies to any civil action or proceeding in which the plaintiff or defendant at the time of filing an application under this section——
>
> (1) is in military service or is within 90 days after termination of or release from military service; and
>
> (2) has received notice of the action or proceeding.

[131] *In re* Ehlke's Estate, 27 N.W.2d 754, 759 (1947).

[132] *In re Cool's Estate*, 18 A.2d 714 at 717.

[133] Barnes v. Winford, 833 P.2d 756, 758 (Colo. App. 1991).

[134] *In re* Ehlke's Estate, 27 N.W.2d at 759.

[135] *See* State of Alaska *ex rel.* Dew v. Superior Court, 907 P.2d 14 (Alaska 1995) (providing a discussion of this point).

[136] This is not to say that distance from the proceeding will necessitate a stay, but merely a brief comment on the law's obvious utility.

[137] *See* 50 U.S.C.S. app. § 531(b) (LEXIS 2006) (stays of evictions and distress proceedings); *id.* app. § 532 (c)(2) (stays of repossession actions under installment contracts); *id.* app. § 533(b) (stays of mortgage foreclosures); *id.* app. § 591 (stays of contract enforcement).

[138] *Id.* § 522.

(b) Stay of proceedings.
  (1) Authority for stay. At any stage before final judgment in a civil action or proceeding in which a servicemember described in subsection (a) is a party, the court may on its own motion and shall, upon application by the servicemember, stay the action for a period of not less than 90 days, if the conditions in paragraph (2) are met.
  (2) Conditions for stay. An application for a stay under paragraph (1) shall include the following:
    (A) A letter or other communication setting forth facts stating the manner in which current military duty requirements materially affect the servicemember's ability to appear and stating a date when the servicemember will be available to appear.
    (B) A letter or other communication from the servicemember's commanding officer stating that the servicemember's current military duty prevents appearance and that military leave is not authorized for the servicemember at the time of the letter.
(c) Application not a waiver of defenses. An application for a stay under this section does not constitute an appearance for jurisdictional purposes and does not constitute a waiver of any substantive or procedural defense (including a defense relating to lack of personal jurisdiction).
(d) Additional stay.
  (1) Application. A servicemember who is granted a stay of a civil action or proceeding under subsection (b) may apply for an additional stay based on continuing material affect of military duty on the servicemember's ability to appear. Such an application may be made by the servicemember at the time of the initial application under subsection (b) or when it appears that the servicemember is unavailable to prosecute or defend the action. The same information required under subsection (b)(2) shall be included in an application under this subsection.
  (2) Appointment of counsel when additional stay refused. If the court refuses to grant an additional stay of proceedings under paragraph (1), the court shall appoint counsel to represent the servicemember in the action or proceeding.
(e) Coordination with section 201. A servicemember who applies for a stay under this section and is unsuccessful may not seek the protections afforded by section 201.
(f) Inapplicability to section 301. The protections of this section do not apply to section 301.[138]

B. Stay Basics

Stays of civil proceedings are available to those in the military service; that is, those who serve on active duty at the time of a court hearing. The protection is exclusive to

[139] Jusino v. New York City Housing Authority, 255 A.D.2d 41, 691 N.Y.S.2d 12 (N.Y. App. Div.

them and not available to dependents[139] and others.[140] This can, nonetheless, come up as an issue and some courts have not been quite as restrictive. Stated differently, if the servicemember is neither the plaintiff nor the defendant, does this mean that his associates who are not in the military can seek the protection of the Act? The answer to the question depends to a large part on the legal relationship of the servicemember not only to the issue in controversy, but also to the parties involved. One court has held that co-makers of a note are entitled to a stay based on the military service of one of the co-makers.[141] Other courts have reached the opposite conclusion, however, in the following situations: when defendant's counsel was unavailable because of military service;[142] when witnesses were unavailable because of military service;[143] and in the case of an auto accident, when the defendant, supervising driver, was negligent, at the time of the accident, in supervising the now absent co-defendant driver who had been driving on a learners' permit.[144]

In contrast to the default protections, the stay protection is applicable to proceedings where the servicemember has notice of the proceeding.[145] This is an important point because it sets up the stay protection as an alternative approach that servicemembers may take. It is applicable whether the servicemember is a plaintiff or a defendant.[146] In comparison, under the default protections the servicemember will ordinarily be the defendant in the proceeding, although it is possible that a plaintiff could suffer a default for lack of appearance on a counterclaim, or perhaps the original plaintiff/petitioner in a case might suffer a default later on a motion to modify.[147]

In order to obtain a stay, a servicemember must send "a letter or other communication" to the court explaining to the court how the servicemember's "military duty requirements materially affect the servicemember's ability to appear"[148] and stating "when the servicemember will be available to appear."[149] *Also*, the servicemember's request must include a letter or other communication from her/his commander[150] stating that the servicemember's current military duty prevents appearance and "that military leave is not authorized."[151]

1999).

[140] Heck v. Anderson, 12 N.W.2d 849 (1944). *But see* Semler v. Oertwig, 12 N.W.2d 265 (1943).

[141] *See* 50 U.S.C. app. § 513; Hempstead Bank v. Gould, 282 N.Y.S.2d 602 (1967). *See also supra* para. 3-7a.

[142] Grimes v. State of Oklahoma, 377 P.2d 847 (1963).

[143] Moulder v. State, 162 S.E.2d 785 (1968).

[144] Forker v. Pomponio, 158 A.2d 849 (1960).

[145] 50 U.S.C. app. § 522(a)(2) (LEXIS 2006).

[146] *Id.* app. § 522(a).

[147] *See supra* para. 3-4a(7).

[148] 50 U.S.C. app. § 522(b)(2)(A).

[149] *Id.*

[150] *Id.* app. § 522(b)(2)(B).

[151] *Id.*

[152] Under the former legislation leave was not mentioned in the statute, but it was, nevertheless, in

Although the commander does not have to provide any further explanation, relate facts nor set a date for when the servicemember can attend, it would be best if the commander elaborated on the facts and, if known, set out a date for the servicemember's attendance. Similarly, regardless of the statute's actual requirements, a statement from the servicemember about leave availability is probably in order.[152]

As to the other basic criteria, the request for the stay can come while the servicemember is on a tour of military service or "within 90 days after termination of or release from military service."[153] Thus, like many SCRA protections, this one extends beyond the time the servicemember is on active duty. As noted the court must grant the request when it comes from the servicemember, but it can do it on its own when it is otherwise aware that the servicemember, with notice, is in the military service.[154] In the event the servicemember's military duty continues to affect his/her ability to attend to the matter, the servicemember can ask for an additional stay with proof of the same sort that would lead to an initial 90-day stay.[155]

Some other basic matters include that the other party should be given notice and an opportunity to be heard on the stay request.[156]

the foreground. Failure by the servicemember to demonstrate that he requested leave and was turned down, or that he had no leave available was usually fatal to a stay request. *See, e.g.*, Hibbard v. Hibbard, 431 N.W.2d 637 (Neb. 1988) (soldier failed to use thirty-eight-day stateside leave to resolve pending support modification motion). *See also*; Bowman v. May, 678 So.2d 1135 (Ala. Civ. App. 1996) (servicemember-plaintiff did not try to get leave or otherwise proceed with cause of action); Underhill v. Barnes, 288 S.E.2d 905 (1982) (when soldier made no showing of attempt to request leave, court took judicial notice of military leave statute to assume Soldier had 50 days of leave accrued based upon length of service); Zaki v. Bryan, 403 N.Y.S.2d 765 (N.Y. App. Div. 1978) (noting entitlement to thirty days leave); Judkins v. Judkins, 441 S.E.2d 139, 142 (1994) (trial court found that servicemember "has failed to exercise good faith and proper diligence in appearing and resolving his case"); and Palo v. Palo, 299 N.W.2d 577, 579 (S.D. 1980) (no stay where servicemember husband "failed to show that he was unable to obtain leave, but he also failed to show that he had even tried to obtain leave"). In tongue-in-cheek fashion, one court denied a stay where the servicemember had not sought leave and where his attorney had asserted that the case could not go forward until after the servicemember had completed a career in the Army and "until we are well into the 21st century." Ensley v. Carter, 538 S.E.2d 98, 100 n.1 (2000). On the other hand, servicemembers who could not obtain leave should be awarded the stay. Keefe v. Spangenberg, 533 F. Supp. 49 (W.D. Ok. 1981) (court would not grant stay for entirety of servicemember's training but would until he finished training and was otherwise able to obtain leave); Allen v. Howard, 384 S.E.2d 894 (1989) (abuse of discretion for trial court to deny request where Sailor could not obtain leave while attending military training); Hawkins v. Hawkins, 999 S.W.2d 171 (Tex. App. 1999).

[153] 50 U.S.C. app. § 522(a)(1) (LEXIS 2006).

[154] *Id.* app. § 522(b)(1).

[155] *Id.* app. § 522(d).

[156] City of Cedartown v. Pickett, 22 S.E.2d 318 (1942); Gunnells v. Searboard A. R. Co., 204 S.E.2d 324 (1974); *see also* Howard v. Howard, 48 S.E.2d 451, 452-3 (1948) (motion for stay should not be *ex parte* and neither should motion to vacate).

[157] In fact, the leading case is probably the Supreme Court case, *Boone v. Lightner*, 319 U.S. 561

C. Material Effect

Before addressing some of the more technical aspects of this protection, it should be noted that material effect is a recurring concept throughout much of the SCRA. As far as the right to a stay of proceedings goes, it is the central issue.[157] Looked at a bit differently, the concept means that "[t]he act cannot be construed to require a continuance on a mere showing that the defendant is in the military service."[158] In general, a servicemember who is being sued in a court a mile from his duty station and residence should be able to make most trial dates just as any other citizen, unless that soldier is out of the area for temporary duty, deployed, or on a field training exercise.[159]

As a preliminary matter, it is immaterial that a delay or inconvenience may result from a stay. A stay is "a proper imposition by the state upon an individual citizen in the course of its discharge of its constitutional obligation to 'provide for the common defense.'"[160] On the other hand, the section cannot be used by a party to shield wrong-

(1943). As is often noted, the Court stated that "[t]he Soldiers' and Sailors' Civil Relief Act is always to be liberally construed to protect those who have been obliged to drop their own affairs to take up the burdens of the nation." *Id.* at 575. It should be noted, however, that the Court also outlined the analysis that other courts have followed when determining whether a stay is warranted. Ironically, the case involved an attorney and the Court did not find a stay was warranted; that is that the service had materially affected the servicemember's ability to litigate the case. To the contrary "[i]nstead of seeking the first competent forum and the earliest possible day to lay his accounts out for vindication, he sought to escape the forum and postpone the day." *Id.*

[158] Hibbard v. Hibbard, 431 N.W.2d 637, 639-40 (Neb. 1988). *See also* Hackman v. Postel, 675 F. Supp. 1132, 1134 (E.D. Ill. 1988 ("mere contentions of unavailability, without affirmative representations that leave to attend the trail was sought by the serviceman and refused, are insufficient to warrant the imposition of relief").

[159] Consider the following recitation:

> Here, . . . the movant resided in the county where the suit was brought. His work was in the environs of the same city. It did not take all of his time. He was able to be present and testify, not only at the trial, but at two other hearings. The case was stayed under his plea for over 18 months. He was able to secure depositions from witnesses in California during that time (the inaccessibility of these witnesses being one of his grounds of application). So far as the record shows, he made no application to the military authorities for leave of absence in order to obtain additional time to prepare his defense in this case.

Brown v. Brown, 437,80 S.E.2d 2, 8 (1953). *Compare* Cox v. Yates, 100 S.E.2d 649 (1957). *See also* Foster v. Alexander, 431 S.E.2d 415 (1993) (court set matter for trial following servicemember return from overseas assignment). In addition to distance, the servicemember's ability to obtain leave is often a relevant, if not determining, factor. *See, e.g.*, Phelps v. Fowler, 688 N.E.2d 558, 562 (1995) ("The affidavit disclosed no attempt to obtain leave, nor did it disclose that the defendant spoke to his commanding officer or the judge advocate general officer concerning leave"). *See also supra* note 152.

[160] Semler v. Oertwig, 12 N.W.2d 265, 269 (1943).

[161] *See Cox*, 100 S.E.2d at 652 ("The act is to be given a liberal construction in favor of soldiers and

doing or lack of diligence,[161] or be used as an instrument by which one in the military service may endanger the peace, health, and lives of people by staying proceedings intended to protect the general public.[162]

In construing the former SSCRA stay provision, several courts have interpreted the question as one that resides within the sound discretion of the trial court. Questions about what constitutes material effect are certainly open for the courts to determine. That is where their discretion comes in and that is where the inquiry should focus.[163]

Congress' thoughts on material effect are, nonetheless, enlightening:

> Stays *should be automatic* if they meet several criteria which adequately place the court on notice when a case may proceed. First, [50 U.S.C. app. § 522] would place an obligation on the servicemember to demonstrate material effect [sic] by providing a factual basis for supporting the stay request. *See Boone* v. *Lightner*, 319 U.S. 561 (1943) (trial courts must use discretion in determining material effect [sic] based on facts presented); *Plesniak* v. *Wiegand*, 31 Ill. 3d 923, 335 N.E. 2d 131 (Ill. App. Ct. 1st District 1975) (party must establish that military status is proximate cause of inability to appear); *Lackey* v. *Lackey*, 222 Va. 49, 278 S.E. 2d 811 (Va. 1981) (affidavit from the commander revealing sailor was serving sea duty and unable to attend sufficient to establish right to a stay); *Hibbard* v. *Hibbard*, 230 Neb. 364, 431 N.W. 2d 637 (Neb. 1988) (determination of a stay depends upon the facts and circumstances of each case). An important component of this requirement would be the servicemember's responsibility to provide a date on which the he or she

sailors to be protected thereby, but it should not be used as an instrument of oppression or a means of defeating an orderly and expeditious trial"). *See also In re* Burrell, 230 B.R. 309, 313 (Bankr. E.D. Tex. 1999) (servicemember "wholly failed to present any evidence"); Riley v. White, 563 So.2d 1039 (Ala. Civ. App. 1990) (stay denied where Soldier failed to voluntarily submit to paternity test before going overseas, after having been granted a previous continuance by court to get tested); Hibbard v. Hibbard, 431 N.W.2d. 637 (1988) (servicemember who refuses to obey court visitation orders and is in contempt of court is not entitled to a stay in change of custody action); Judkins v. Judkins, 441 S.E.2d 139 (1994) (stay denied when Soldier received several continuances and stays because of military duty in Persian Gulf conflict, but upon return refused to comply with court discovery orders).

[162] Technically, neither the SSCRA nor the SCRA exclude any type of administrative or civil matter from their reach. Still, there are a few reported decisions which seem to indicate that certain matters are beyond the scope. *See, e.g.*, Baskin v. Meadors, 27 S.E.2d 696 (1943 (public nuisance); *City of Cedartown* **need citation here** (case involving public nuisance outside the SSCRA's reach); State *ex rel.* Swanson v. Heaton, 22 N.W.2d 815 (1946) (public nuisance).

[163] *See, e.g.*, Coburn v. Coburn, 412 So.2d 947 (Fla. Ct. App. 1982) (trial court abuse of discretion). *Compare* Power v. Power, 720 S.W.2d 683 (Tex. Ct. App. 1986) (mere statement that party is in the military service is insufficient).

[164] H.R. Rep. No. 108-81, at 38 (2003) (emphasis added).

> would be available to appear. *See Tabor* v. *Miller*, 389 F. 2d 645, *cert. denied, Stearns* v. *Tabor*, 391 U.S. 915 (3d Cir. 1968) (servicemember did not provide evidence it was impossible for him to appear); *Zitomer* v. *Holdsworth*, 449 F.2d 724 (3d Cir. 1971) (servicemember failed to avail himself of SSCRA provisions).[164]

If a court finds material effect (and that the service member is unavailable to defend), the court must order a stay.[165] If the stay request is denied, a good rule of thumb is for the court to make findings of fact about the lack of material effect, or ensure there is sufficient evidence in the record to warrant denial.[166]

Finally, in deciding whether to grant a stay, a court must consider all the facts and circumstances.[167] This "does not imply a power to stay in anticipating that at some future time in the litigation's progress the ability of the service man to prosecute or defend may be materially affected by reason of his military service."[168]

D. Common Law Rules

While the current statute and its predecessor[169] imply a relatively straightforward inquiry, the courts have been known to inquire into whether the servicemember is a necessary party or otherwise required to attend the proceedings. The inquiry turns, then, on whether the servicemember's case will be prejudiced by his/her absence.

The Court of Appeals of Ohio explained this development in the case of *Olsen v. Olsen*.[170] First, they reasoned that "it was improper to deny a motion to stay proceedings without findings by the court that the soldier's ability to defend is not materially affected by military duties."[171] Obviously, this part of the analysis is based on the

[165] *See, e.g.*, Smith v. Smith, 149 S.E.2d 468, 470 (1966) ("intensive training at Fort Bragg, North Carolina, in preparation for active duty in Viet Nam"); Lackey v. Lackey, 278 S.E.2d 811, 812 (1981) ("trial court erred in denying . . . a continuance . . . [where the servicemember] was serving on board a Navy ship on sea duty and was unable to leave the ship").

[166] Olsen v. Olsen, 621 N.E. 2d 830 (Ohio 1993).

[167] *See, e.g.*, Hibbard v. Hibbard, 431 N.W.2d. 637 (1988)

[168] Sullivan v. Storz, 55 N.W.2d 499, 504 (1952).

[169] The former statute read as follows:

> At any stage thereof any action or proceeding in any court in which a person in military service is involved, either as a plaintiff or defendant, during the period of such service or within sixty days thereafter, may in the discretion of the court in which it is pending, on its own motion, and shall, on application to it by such person or some person on his behalf be stayed as provided in this Act, unless, in the opinion of the court, the ability of plaintiff to prosecute the action or the defendant to conduct his defense is not materially affected by reason of his military service.

50 U.S.C. app. § 521 (2000).

[170] 621 N.E2d 830 (1993).

[171] *Id.* at 830 (citing Coburn v. Coburn, 412 So.2d 947 (Fla. Dist. Ct. App. 1982)).

[172] *Id.* (quoting Mays v. Tharpe & Broooks, Inc., 240 S.E.2d 159 (1977)).

statute. It went on to note, however, that "unless it is a situation in which no harm could accrue by reason of his absence, generally recognized as an exception in the statute, a member of the military service is entitled as of right to the stay."[172]

It is one thing to determine that a servicemember is not a necessary party. There is also some logic to this rule even though it does extend beyond the statutory language. If a party's presence is unnecessary, then there is no need to reach the question about whether or not the person's circumstances (military duties) preclude attendance. For example, the Mississippi Supreme Court found a military father was not a necessary party in a child custody proceeding involving the mother and the children's paternal grandmother.[173] It is another thing, however, for a case to turn on a consideration of the substance of the proceeding rather than on the question about whether the servicemember's duty materially affects his/her ability to attend. For example, there is a line of cases indicating that in a personal injury case, it is the insurance company and not the insured servicemember who is the real party in interest.[174]

Consider also the result in the case of *Shelor v. Shelor*.[175] In that case, the Georgia Supreme Court held that temporary modifications of child support do not materially affect the rights of a military defendant as they are "interlocutory and subject to modification."[176] Stated a bit differently, the court said that "his defense . . . is generally not materially affected by determination of the interlocutory relief sought." Even though the courts have created this examination, and even though it has arguable merit, the focus, for SCRA purposes should be on the impact of the servicemember's duty. In *Shelor*, interestingly enough, the servicemember "was apparently at home during the hearing, and the record is void of any evidence concerning the reason for his failure to attend other than his counsel's bare assertion that [the servicemember] was ordered to direct the movers dispatched that day." [177] Thus, looking aside from the substance of the proceeding, the court had a proper ground for its determination.

[173] Bubac v. Boston, 600 So.2d 951 (Miss. 1992).

[174] Underhill v. Barnes, 288 S.E.2d 905, 907 (Ga. Ct. App. 1982); Hackman v. Postel, 675 F. Supp. 1132 (N.D. Ill. 1988). *See also* Murphy v. Wheatley, 360 F.2d 180 (5th Cir. 1966) (subrogation claims where real parties in interest are the insurance companies of the parties). Other substantive questions have been looked at similarly. *See, also*, City of Cedartown v. Pickett, 512-13, 22 S.E.2d 318, 321-2 (1942) (due process violation to fail to serve opponent with request to stay, but alternatively SSCRA inapplicable to suit involving a public nuisance); Foster v. Alexander, 431 S.E.2d 415 (case involving policy limits of automobile insurance policy); Jackson v. Jackson, 403 N.W.2d 248 (Minn. Ct. App. 1987); *But see* Wilson v. Speer, 499 N.W.2d 850, (Minn. Ct. App. 1993) (record in denial of stay in child support case must establish why parent's presence unnecessary); Cornelius v. Jackson, 209 P.2d 166, 170 (1948) ("there was no question of fact involved and . . . the questions involved were questions of law"); *In re* Marriage of Peck, 920 P.2d 236 (1996) (lack of personal jurisdiction could be considered in servicemember's absence). *But see* Starling v. Harris, 151 S.E.2d 163 (1966) (servicemember's "presence was essential to a proper defense to this action in tort arising out of an automobile collision to which there were no eyewitnesses other than the parties and to which action the defendant claimed a good defense").

[175] 383 S.E.2d 895 (1989). *Id.* at 896.

[176] *Id.*

[177] *Id.*

[178] Derby v. Kim, 233 S.E.2d 156, 157-8 (1977) (in child custody case involving question of paren-

On the other end of the spectrum are cases that looked to the substance of the proceeding to seemingly minimize the showing of material effect or otherwise indicating that certain issues inherently require the person's attendance.[178] Ultimately, the question is whether substantive issues and their relative complexity should not determine the outcome. Again, it is one thing to determine that a servicemember has no interest or part in the suit, but care needs to be taken to avoid an outcome where consideration of that point replaces a proper examination the question of material effect. Stated a bit differently, "[a] soldier . . . is not entitled to relief under the Soldiers' and Sailors' Civil Relief Act as a consequence of his membership in the armed services, but, rather, because his defense is materially affected by his military service."[179]

E. Burden of Proof

In the seminal *Boone v. Lightner* decision, the Supreme Court noted that the SSCRA "[made] no express provision as to who must carry the burden of showing that a party will or will not be prejudiced."[180] Nonetheless, the Court stated that "[w]e, too, refrain from declaring any rigid doctrine of burden of proof in this matter, believing that courts called upon to use discretion will usually have enough sound sense to know from what direction their information should be expected to come" and "ultimate discretion includes a discretion as to whom the court may ask to come forward with facts needful to a fair judgment."[181]

Even so, the courts have, from time-to-time, endeavored to refine this point. Some have reasoned that it is squarely on the servicemember.[182] Others place it on the party standing in opposition to the continuance.[183] Others turn to the Supreme Court's *ad hoc* approach.[184] Regardless, given the legislation's current language calling for a "communication setting forth facts,"[185] it is safe to assume that the burden will normally be on the servicemember.

F. Practical Considerations

Although a servicemember may have a right to a stay based on his/her military service, there is a need to be reasonable. Even if a servicemember can obtain a leave of

tal fitness, "it should have been obvious from the nature of the issues to be litigated . . . that the father's presence was important"); Mathis v. Mathis, 236 So.2d 755, 756-7 (Miss. 1970) ("a paternity suit is of such a personal and intimate nature that it is implicit that appellant's absence materially affects his defense unless a specific finding is made to the contrary").

[179] Wilson v. Butler, 584 So.2d 414, 416 (Miss. 1991).

[180] Boone v. Lightner, 319 U.S. 561, 569 (1943).

[181] *Id.* at 569.

[182] *See, e.g.*, *Wilson*, 584 So.2d at 416 (quoting Roberts v. Fuhr, 523 So.2d 20, 28 (Miss. 1987) and Mayfair Sales, Inc. v. Sames, 169 So.2d 150, 152 (La. 1964).

[183] Coburn v. Coburn, 412 So.2d 947 (Fla. App. 1982).

[184] Allfirst Bank v. Lewis (*In re* Lewis), 257 B.R. 431 (Bankr. D. Md. 2001).

[185] 50 U.S.C.S. app. § 522(b)(2)(A) (LEXIS 2006).

[186] *See, e.g.*, Underhill v. Barnes, 288 S.E.2d 905 (1995).

absence, it has to be asked whether the servicemember's presence truly justifies the expense of round trip airfare. On the one hand, distance, leave accrual, and expense are worth considering as a court determines whether to grant a stay,[186] but they are also factors for a servicemember to consider when examining alternative approaches to an impending court proceeding. After all, "the ability to communicate across the Atlantic Ocean has improved from its condition in 1940."[187] The impact of the Internet, video teleconferencing, and video depositions[188] on court determinations as to the unavailability of servicemembers for civil case discovery has yet to be fully realized. Video teleconferencing or Internet contact, however, should not substitute for servicemembers' physical presence at their trial on the merits as[189] "[t]he opponent of the absent party will always have the edge [at trial]."[190] Still, an assessment of the pros and cons of any situation may lead to a conclusion that little is to be gained in delay.

G. Bankruptcy

Another practical consideration that is worth highlighting is the relationship between the stay provision and bankruptcy proceedings. First, the SCRA is applicable to bankruptcy cases.[191] An issue comes up, however, for the simple reason that the movant will often be the bankruptcy petitioner/debtor. There is a noted irony to the fact that bankruptcy, even under the best of circumstances, works to hamper a creditor's rights or to otherwise diminish what the creditor originally contracted for. A delay in resolution can often work to deepen the creditor's disadvantage, turning the SCRA's stay provision into "a sword against creditors rather than a shield."[192]

Notwithstanding this irony and the gloss it may put on a court's treatment, it has to be recognized that the stay provision is applicable to both plaintiffs and defendants.[193] Bankruptcy judges will need to examine the issue of material effect just as they would in any other situation.[194]

[187] Massey v. Kim, 455 S.E.2d 306, 307 (1995).

[188] Keefe v. Spangenberg, 533 F. Supp. 49 (W.D. Okla. 1981) (court denied stay request to delay deposition, and suggested that service member agree to videotape deposition in accordance with Federal Rules of Civil Procedure Rule 30(b)(4)); *see also In re* Diaz, 82 B.R. 162, 165 (Bankr. D. Ga. 1988) (service members in Germany may make video depositions for use in trials in the United States, so Section 201 stay is not appropriate to delay discovery).

[189] Roger M. Baron, *The Staying Power of the Soldiers' and Sailors' Civil Relief Act*, 32 Santa Clara L. Rev. 137, 162 (1992).

[190] *Id.* at 165. *See also* Major Howard McGillin, Note, *Stays of Judicial Proceedings*, Army Law., July 1995, at 68, 69-70.

[191] Duggan v. Franklin Square Nat'l Bank, 170 F.2d 922 (2d Cir. 1948).

[192] *In re* Burrell, 230 B.R. 309, (Bankr. E.D. Tex. 1999).

[193] 50 U.S.C.S. app. § 522(a) (LEXIS 2006).

[194] *Burrell*, 230 B.R. at 313 (no evidence despite servicemember's assignment in Germany). *See also* Allfirst Bank v. Lewis (*In re* Lewis), 257 B.R. 431 (Bankr. D. Md. 2001) (stay granted while servicemember stationed overseas, but matter to move forward given return to continental United States).

[195] 50 U.S.C.S. app. § 522(b)(1).

H. Additional Stays

If a court finds that there has been a proper showing, the SCRA requires that it "shall stay the action for a period of not less than 90 days."[195] When a servicemember requests and is granted a stay, that servicemember may seek a further stay if the situation warrants. The servicemember, that is, "may apply for an additional stay based on the servicemember's ability to appear."[196] In fact, "[t]he same information required [for an initial request for a stay] shall be included in an application [for an additional stay]."[197] Thus, when a court considers this type of request, it should use essentially the same analysis as it would for the initial request.

The most important thing to note about these additional stays, however, is the fact that the court must appoint an attorney if it denies the request.[198] Although this a new requirement brought in by the SCRA, it is not without precedent.[199] As to the attorney's role,[200] the requirement is similar to the appointment of an attorney under the default provisions.[201] Like the default provision, the stay provision states that the attorney is there "to represent the servicemember in the action or proceeding,"[202] but the exact extent of that representation is not defined.

I. Welfare Reform Act Interface

The Welfare Reform Act of 1996[203] mandated that the Department of Defense facilitate leave for servicemembers involved in child custody and paternity disputes. Accordingly, the Department has promulgated an instruction indicating that "ordinary leave shall be granted unless . . . [t]he member is serving in or with a unit deployed in a contingency operation; or . . . [e]xigencies of military service require a denial of such request."[204]

VI. Interface of the Stay Provisions and the Default Protections

For many years, there has been a noted tension between the default and the stay proceeding. Simply put, if a stay request is denied, will the servicemember be barred from challenging the outcome pursuant to the default provisions?[205] In the past, there

[196] *Id.* app. § 522(d)(1).
[197] *Id.*
[198] *Id.* app. § 522(d)(2).
[199] *See, e.g.*, Coburn v. Coburn, 412 So.2d 947 (Fla. App. 1982).
[200] *See supra* para. 3-4b for a discussion of the appointed attorney's role under the default protections provision.
[201] 50 U.S.C. app. § 521(b)(2).
[202] *Id.*
[203] Pub. L. No. 104-193, 110 Stat. 2105 (1996).
[204] U.S. Dep't of Defense, Instr. 1326.7, Leave and Liberty Procedures para. 6.22 (22 Apr. 2005).
[205] *See, e.g.*, McGillin, *supra* note 190. Major Garth K. Chandler, *The Impact of a Request for a Stay of Proceedings Under the Solders' and Sailors' Civil Relief Act*, 102 Mil. L. Rev. 169, 171 (1983).

may have been ways to ask for the continuance, to see it denied and to come back later and successfully set aside a default judgment. There may have been courts willing to allow a request for a continuance as a special pleading and not as a waiver of all defenses,[206] but the best advice was probably as follows:

> Where the service member learns of a default judgment after it has been entered, he or she should immediately obtain counsel and make application to have the judgment opened. If he or she had been truly unaware of the action, there should be little trouble in getting the judgment opened. His or her ultimate success will, of course, depend on the substantive merits of the case.
>
> Where a service member receives notice of a pending action, he or she should immediately enter an appearance and defend. If military duties interfere with the ability to defend, the service member should seek every avenue to be permitted to attend to the court's action. Failing this, a stay of proceedings . . . should be sought. The service member risks denial or [sic] the request and subsequent loss of the right to a court-appointed attorney and may even lose the right to open a default judgment as a result of this appearance. Yet, little is really lost.[207]

With the adoption of the SCRA, Congress appears to want to see litigation channeled in accordance with this viewpoint. They are firm in their confirmation that an unsuccessful request for a stay will preclude resort to the default protections.[208] Thus, when a servicemember has notice of a proceeding, that servicemember will have to decide whether to enter an appearance, attempt to be released from duty to defend, and to defend or whether to await a default judgment and attempt to reopen it at a more convenient time.

It should be noted, however, that Congress tempered this outcome. Implicit in the historical tension between the two choices was the notion that an entry of appearance might work to waive certain defenses. A request for a continuance might work as an entry of appearance and not only preclude later resort to the default protections, but also waive certain otherwise valid defenses that the servicemember would want to protect if s/he could only get to the courthouse. Now, Congress has hopefully allayed this fear by indicating that "[a]n application for a stay . . . does not constitute an appearance for jurisdictional purposes and does not constitute a waiver of any substantive or procedural defense (including a defense relating to lack of personal jurisdiction)."[209]

[206] O'Neill v. O'Neill, 515 So.2d 1208 (Miss. 1987). *But see* Skates v. Stockton, 683 P.2d 304 (Ariz. App. 1984).
[207] *Chandler*, *supra* note 205, at 178.
[208] 50 U.S.C.S. app. § 522(e) (LEXIS 2006).
[209] *Id.* app. § 522(c).

Finally, if the servicemember is not immediately available and not in a position to hire counsel, explore a defense, request a stay and otherwise begin to defend, in other words, when the servicemember is about to be defaulted against, the court must look to stay the proceeding for 90 days before entering the default judgment.[210] The default protections include, up front, protection that means to allow the servicemember every opportunity to defend.

VII. Persons Liable on Servicemember's Obligation

A. Persons Who Are Primarily and Secondarily Liable with Servicemember

Subsections 513(a) and 513(b) provide those persons who are either primarily or secondarily liable with a servicemember on an obligation or liability with the same rights to delay actions and vacate judgments available to servicemembers.

50 U.S.C. app. § 513(a)-(b)

(a) Extension of protection when actions stayed, postponed, or suspended. Whenever pursuant to this Act a court stays, postpones, or suspends (1) the enforcement of an obligation or liability, (2) the prosecution of a suit or proceeding, (3) the entry or enforcement of an order, writ, judgment, or decree, or (4) the performance of any other act, the court may likewise grant such a stay, postponement, or suspension to a surety, guarantor, endorser, accommodation maker, comaker, or other person who is or may be primarily or secondarily subject to the obligation or liability the performance or enforcement of which is stayed, postponed, or suspended.

(b) Vacation or set—aside of judgments. When a judgment or decree is vacated or set aside, in whole or in part, pursuant to this Act, the court may also set aside or vacate, as the case may be, the judgment or decree as to a surety, guarantor, endorser, accommodation maker, comaker, or other person who is or may be primarily or secondarily liable on the contract or liability for the enforcement of the judgment or decree.[211]

Specifically, these subsections allow the court in its discretion to grant stays, postponements, or suspensions of suits or proceedings to sureties, guarantors, endorsers, accommodation makers, and others.

Sureties and others may find that obtaining a stay is not always easy. For example, a Georgia court held that where liability is joint and several and the action is brought against an accessible civilian party, the proceedings will not be stayed unless the servicemember is a party to the action.[212] Similarly, in *Modern Industrial Bank v. Zaentz*,[213] the court specified that co-obligors are entitled to a stay only if the

[210] *See id.* app. § 521(d).
[211] *Id.* app. § 513.
[212] Hartsfield Co. v. Whitfield, 30 S.E.2d 648 (1944).
[213] 29 N.Y.S.2d 969 (N.Y. City Mun. Ct. 1941).

servicemember is a party to the action and the action has been stayed as to the servicemember. Finally, the right to open a judgment taken against a person in the military service is reserved to that person only and not to a judgment co-debtor.[214]

Other courts have been less interested in the servicemember's status with respect to the litigation.[215] In exercising their discretion "the courts are primarily influenced by two considerations: first, whether the man in service is able to appear and defend, and second, whether a default on an obligation by reason of the change in his income will lead to an unjust forfeiture."[216]

B. Codefendants

As previously indicated, a proceeding stayed as to a servicemember may also be stayed as to others primarily or secondarily subject to the same liability. In Section 525,[217] however, the Act allows a court to proceed against other codefendants, notwithstanding a stay as to the servicemember. These codefendants are not among those sureties, guarantors, and so on covered by Section 513.

A Washington state appellate court was presented with the problem of a servicemember driving a vehicle owned by his father. They were named as codefendants in a negligence action. The incident giving rise to the suit was witnessed only by the plaintiff and the absent servicemember/son. The trial court stayed the proceedings as to the son but denied a stay to the father, who was independently liable under the doctrine of imputed negligence. The appellate court held that the denial was within the trial court's discretion.[218]

C. Criminal Bail Bond Sureties

The SCRA offers no protection to the criminal defendant. For example, the law's stay provisions[219] are inapplicable to criminal proceedings. There is, however, some relief with respect to bail bonds and those who serve as sureties for a defendant in military service. The language of subsection 513(c) prescribes that the "court may not enforce a bail bond during the period of military service of the principal on the bond when military service prevents the surety from obtaining the attendance of the principal."[220] Furthermore, "[t]he court may discharge the surety and exonerate the bail in accor-

[214] J.C. Penney v. Oberpriller, 163 S.W.2d 1067 (Tex. Civ. App. 1942), *rev'd on other grounds*, 170 S.W.2d 607 (1943).

[215] *See, e.g.*, Akron Auto Fin. Co. v. Stonebraker, 35 N.E.2d585 (1941).

[216] Note, 9 U. CHI. L. REV. 348, 349 (1942).

[217] 50 U.S.C.S. app. § 525 (LEXIS 2006).

[218] State *ex rel.* Frank v. Bunge, 133 P.2d 515 91943).

[219] 50 U.S.C. app. § 522.

[220] *Id.* § 513(c).

dance with the principals of equity and justice, during or after the period of military service of the principal."[221]

Illustrative of these provisions' application is the case of *United States v. Jeffries*.[222] In that case, the court held that there was no doubt that the principal was in the military. Because of this, it was without authority to forfeit the bail bond and issue a warrant of arrest. Former 50 U.S.C. app. § 513(3) was held to be mandatory.[223] The modern provision's language is no less clear indicating that "[a] court may not enforce a bail bond during the period of military service of the principal on the bond when military service prevents the surety from obtaining the attendance of the principal."[224] In a latter case, a New York court took this one step further, holding that the bond could not be forfeited if the principal was in the service even if he were on furlough at the time he was required to appear.[225]

In *Ex Parte Moore*,[226] however, an Alabama court concluded that military service alone was insufficient to prevent forfeiture of the bail bond without a further showing that military service prevented the principal from attending the trial.[227] Courts echoing

[221] *Id.* In what may be an anomaly, the Arkansas Supreme Court held, in *dicta*, that the surety must show three things. The court said "the surety is not entitled to relief in the absence of a showing that the principal was in the military service on the date he was scheduled to appear, that the surety made an unsuccessful effort to secure [the principal's] appearance on that date and that [the principal's] military service prevented his attendance on that date." Tri-State Bonding Co. v. State, 567 S.W.2d 937, 942 (1978). The court did not resolve the issue on this ground, however. Instead, the judgment against the surety came because the issue had not been properly raised and preserved. *Id.* The dissent seemed more willing to found its opinion on the plain statutory language and fact that the principal had been serving with the Army in Georgia on the day of trial. *Id.* at 946.

[222] 140 F.2d 745 (7th Cir. 1944).

[223] *Id.*

[224] 50 U.S.C. app. § 513(c). In comparison to the former provision, the modern language is clearer. The former provision stated that "[w]henever by reason of military service of a principal upon a criminal bail bond the sureties upon such bond are prevented from enforcing the attendance of their principal and performing their obligation the court shall not enforce the provisions of such bond during the military service of the principal." 50 U.S.C. app. § 513(3) (2000).

[225] People v. Correa, 43 N.Y.S.2d 266 (1943).

[226] 12 So.2d 77 (1943).

[227] This case should be read with caution because, as the court notes, the SSCRA provision in question "was approved after the conditional judgment [forfeiting the bond] was here rendered." *Id.* at 77. In fact, the *Moore* court was most concerned to note that a bond forfeiture results in a final, appealable judgment and that a petition for a writ of mandamus would be inappropriate. *See, e.g.*, Esensoy v. Board of Pardons & Paroles, 793 So.2d 744 (Ala. 2000); State v. Cobb, 264 So.2d 523, 525 (1972) ("It is established that mandamus will not be granted where petitioner has adequate remedy by appeal"). On the other hand, other cases have noted these aspects in *Moore* and still found that more is required for the surety to salvage the bond. *See, e.g.*, State v. Benedict, 15 N.W.2d 248, 251 (1944).

this outcome will require the surety show that the principal is in the military and demonstrate an effort to secure the principal's attendance.[228]

In cases in which the principal was discharged four months before default and forfeiture[229] or where the principal was not inducted until almost six months after he was required to appear,[230] the surety will have little hope for relief. As one court held, "[the surety is] provided a legal defense . . . while the principal was in the military service of the United States."[231]

VIII. Stay or Vacation of Execution of Judgments, Attachments

Section 524 is another "stay" section of the Act:

> 50 U.S.C. app. § 524
>
> (a) Court action upon material effect determination. If a servicemember, in the opinion of the court, is materially affected by reason of military service in complying with a court judgment or order, the court may on its own motion and shall on application by the servicemember—
> (1) stay the execution of any judgment or order entered against the servicemember; and
> (2) vacate or stay an attachment or garnishment of property, money, or debts in the possession of the servicemember or a third party, whether before or after judgment.
>
> (b) Applicability. This section applies to an action or proceeding commenced in a court against a servicemember before or during the period of the servicemember's military service or within 90 days after such service terminates.[232]

A. General

Section 524 differs from other stay provisions because it is not a stay of proceedings, but authorizes a court to stay execution of a judgment or order entered against a servicemember. It also authorizes a court to vacate or stay an attachment or garnishment on a servicemember's property. The same basic rules for granting stays under section 522 apply to section 524. Servicemembers must act in good faith. Their military service must materially affect their ability to comply with the judgment or decree entered against them. The suit giving rise to the judgment may have commenced prior to, during, or within 90 days after military service.

[228] *See, e.g.*, People v. Cont'l Cas. Co., 134 N.Y.S.2d 742 (1954) ("surety must also demonstrate that it made an unsuccessful effort to secure the person of the principal from the military authorities"); Cumbie v. State, 367 S.W.2d 693 (Tex. Civ. App. 1963).

[229] United States v. Carolina Cas. Ins. Co., 237 F.2d 451 (7'h Cir. 1956).

[230] State v. Benedict, 15 N.W.2d 248 (1944).

[231] *Carolina Cas. Ins. Co.*, 237 F.2d at 453.

There have been only a few reported decisions addressing the statute's predecessor. Those that have, discuss the matter along lines very similar to ordinary stays. For example, the courts are vested with a degree of discretion in deciding what constitutes material effect[233] and a mere showing that the person is in or is now in the military service is not sufficient.[234]

B. Department of Defense Directive 1344.9

This section does not apply to actions to involuntarily allot military pay to civil creditors pursuant to Department of Defense Directive 1344.9,[235] and Department of Defense Instruction 1344.12.[236] These involuntary allotments are not court-ordered executions or garnishments, and thus this section will not stay enforcement of such an involuntary allotment for non-marital debts.

IX. Tolling of the Statue of Limitations

50 U.S.C. app. § 526

Another significant procedural protection is the provision tolling the running of the statute of limitations:

> (a) Tolling of statutes of limitation during military service. The period of a servicemember's military service may not be included in computing any period limited by law, regulation, or order for the bringing of any action or proceeding in a court, or in any board, bureau, commission, department, or other agency of a State (or political subdivision of a State) or the United States by or against the servicemember or the servicemember's heirs, executors, administrators, or assigns.
>
> (b) Redemption of real property. A period of military service may not be included in computing any period provided by law for the redemption of real property sold or forfeited to enforce an obligation, tax, or assessment.
>
> (c) Inapplicability to internal revenue laws. This section does not apply to any period of limitation prescribed by or under the internal revenue laws of the United States.[237]

[232] 50 U.S.C.S. app. § 524 (LEXIS 2006).

[233] *See, e.g.*, Halstead v. Halstead, 165 P.2d 513 (1946); McKinney v. McKinney, 50 N.Y.S.2d 8 (N.Y. Sup. Ct. 1944).

[234] *See, e.g.*, Pope v. United States Fid. & Guar. Co., 20 S.E.2d 618 (1942).

[235] U.S. Dep't of Defense, Dir. 1344.9, Indebtedness of Military Personnel (27 Oct 1994) [Hereinafter DoD Dir. 1344.9].

[236] U.S. Dep't of Defense, Instr. 1344.12, Indebtedness Processing Procedures for Military Personnel (18 Nov. 1994) [hereinafter DoD Instr. 1344.12].

[237] 50 U.S.C.S. app. § 526.

This section of the Act tolls statutes of limitation during the period of military service of any military plaintiff or defendant and "once [military service] . . . is shown, the period of limitations is automatically tolled for the duration of the service."[238] The courts have held that this section is applicable to state[239] and municipal governments.[240] It applies in probate,[241] bankruptcy[242] and administrative proceedings[243] to include actions before the boards of correction of military records[244] and matters before the Merit Systems Protection Board.[245] Whether the cause of action accrued prior to or during the period of service is immaterial.[246] This section is inapplicable, however, to periods of limitations imposed by federal internal revenue laws.[247]

Unlike other general relief provisions, section 526 does not require that servicemembers show their military service materially affected their ability to participate in the proceedings. Although there had been some confusion over this point in the past, the Supreme Court said, in a case involving a career servicemember, that "[t]he

[238] Ricard v. Birch, 529 F.2d 214, 2117 (4th Cir. 1975). *But see*, *In re* Sarah C. v. Paul D., 11 Cal. Rptr.2d 414 (1992) (court seems to add an additional, and questionable, requirement that the servicemember seek a stay rather than seek relief simply under the tolling provision). *See also In re* Melicia L. v. Raymond L., 254 Cal. Rptr. 541 (1988).
[239] Parker v. State, 57 N.Y.S.2d 242 (Ct. Cl. 1945).
[240] Calderon v. City of New York, 55 N.Y.S.2d 674 (Sup. Ct. 1945).
[241] State *ex rel.* Estate of Perry v. Roper, 168 S.W.3d 577 (Mo. Ct. App. 2005).
[242] Baxter v. Watson (*In re* Watson), 292 B.R. 441, (Bankr. S.D. Ga. 2003; A.H. Robins Co., Inc. v. Dalkon Shield Claimants Trust, 996 F.2d 716 (4th Cir. 1993).
[243] Shell Oil Co. v. Indus. Comm'n, 94 N.E.2d 888 (1950).
[244] Detweiler v. Pena, 38 F 3d 591 (D.C.Cir., 1994). *Accord* Hanes v. United States, 44 Fed. Cl. 441 (1999); Kosnik v. Peters, 31 F. Supp.2d 151 (D. D.C. 1998); Ortiz v. Sec'y of Defense, 41 F.3d 738 (D.C. Cir. 1994); There is, however, some lingering "debate" about the applicability of the SCRA's tolling provision to the boards of correction statute of limitations. Randall v. United States, 95 F.3d 339, 341 n.3 (4th Cir. 1996). *See also* Mouradian v. John Hancock Cos., 930 F.2d 972 (1st Cir. 1991), *cert. denied*, 503 U.S. 951 (1992) (more specific military tolling provision in National Labor Relations Act requiring showing of material effect held applicable instead of former SSCRA tolling provision).
[245] Davis v. Dep't of the Air Force, 51 M.S.P.R 246 (1991).
[246] Oberlin v. United States, 727 F.Supp. 946 (E.D. Penn. 1989); *In re* Thompson v. Reedman, 201 F. Supp. 837 (E.D. Pa. 1961); Wolf's Estate, 264 F.2d 82 (3rd Cir. 1959).
[247] 50 U.S.C. app. § 526(c) (LEXIS 2006). *See also* Stone v. C.I.R., 73 T.C. 617 (1980). Even those revenue laws benefiting taxpayers, such as those allowing for claims for overpayments, are not tolled. *See, e.g.*, Allen v. United States, 439 F. Supp. 463 (D.C. Cal. 1977).

statutory command . . . is unambiguous, unequivocal, and unlimited."[248] In other words, the servicemember need make no showing that the military service has materially affected his or her ability to bring a cause of action and the protection is available to career servicemembers.[249]

Notwithstanding the Supreme Court's statements on this point, there is the possibility that the other party will succeed on a claim of laches.[250] In these cases, the court "must have indications of both elements of laches—inexcusable delay in filing suit and prejudice resulting to defendant."[251]

Section 526 can, of course, be a two-edged sword. It can operate both to the advantage and to the disadvantage of a servicemember because it applies to actions by or against the servicemember.[252] It is not applicable to suits involving family members

[248] Conroy v. Aniskoff, 507 U.S. 511, 514 (1993). The issue in the case revolved around a career servicemember who failed to pay taxes on real estate and who then failed to seek the property's redemption. *Id.* at 513. Although holding that the former SSCRA's tolling provision worked to the servicemember's advantage, the Court did remark that "we are confident that Congress would have corrected the injustice—or will do so in the future." *Id.* at 518. Thus, it is interesting to compare the older provision with the modern, SCRA, version. Under the prior legislation, the statute stated that "nor shall any part of such [military service] period which occurs after 6 October 1942 be included in computing any period now or hereafter provided by any law for the redemption of real property sold or forfeited to enforce any obligation, tax, or assessment." 50 U.S.C. app. § 525 (2000). Congress obviously felt it was being anything but unfair as the new provision explains that "[a] period of military service may not be included in computing any period provided by law for the redemption of real property sold or forfeited to enforce an obligation, tax, or assessment." 50 U.S.C.S. app. § 526(b) (LEXIS 2006). The general tolling provisions have also changed very little. *Compare id.* app. § 526(a), *with* 50 U.S.C. app. § 525 (2000).

[249] In *Conroy*, the Supreme Court not only overruled the Maine Supreme Court, but indicated its specifically its disapproval of certain decisions which had felt there was a need for career servicemembers to show material effect. *See Conroy*, 511 U.S. at 514 n.4 (citing Pannell v. Continental Can Co., 554 F.2d 216 (5th Cir. 1977)); Bailey v. Barranca, 488 P.2d 725 (1971); King v. Zagorski, 207 So.2d 61 (Fla. App. 1968).

[250] Detweiler v. Pena, 38 F 3d 591 (D.C.Cir., 1994). *See also* Neptune v. United States, 38 Fed. Cl. 510 (1997).

[251] Deering v. United States, 620 F.2d 242, 245 (1980) (despite tolling, laches proved). *See also* Cornetta v. United States, 851 F.2d 1372 (Fed. Cir. 1988) (laches not proved); (Foster v. United States, 733 F.2d 88 (Fed. Cir. 1984) (laches proved). Many cases dealing with laches and the former tolling provisions revolve around military pay claims and the like, but the doctrine of laches has been applied notwithstanding the tolling provision in the context of purely civilian controversies. *See, e.g.*, Landis v. Hodgson, 706 P.2d 1363 (Ida. App. 1985).

[252] *See* Ricard v. Birch, 529 F.2d 214, 216 (4th Cir. 1975) ("the parallel purpose of the Act [is] to protect the rights of individuals having causes of action against members of the armed forces"). *See also* Hamner v. BMY Combat Sys. 869 F. Supp. 888 (D. Kan., 1994), *aff'd*, 79 F.3d 1156 (10th Cir. 1996) (suit dismissed where injured servicemember files suit 2 years and one day after release from active duty, one day after running of two year statute of limitations).

and their claims.[253] While the statute's "heirs, executors, administrators, or assigns"[254] language may be of utility to a servicemember's estate, it does not work to extend the protection to family members.[255]

Courts may also decide that the time period in question is not actually a statute of limitation.[256] In addition, the provision only applies to the time period before bringing a suit. It does not extend time periods within a suit, such as time periods to avoid motions to dismiss for failure to prosecute an action.[257] It is inapplicable if the servicemember has no interest in the suit or proceeding.[258] This provision also applies to Reserve Component active military duty service, but not weekend drill or individual unit training[259] and it is, of course, inapplicable to the National Guard when not in federal service.[260] Although a statute of limitations is tolled during periods of active duty, it has been noted that the SSCRA, like the current SCRA, defines "military service" a bit more broadly. It can also encompass "any period during which a servicemember is absent from duty on account of sickness, wounds, leave, or other lawful cause."[261] Thus, a person who was no longer performing ordinary duties but who "was . . . on the 'temporary disability retired list'" would be covered.[262]

X. Revocation of Interlocutory Orders

A final procedural rule is found in section 583. In straightforward fashion, it provides that "[a]n interlocutory order issued by a court under this Act may be revoked, modified, or extended by that court upon its own motion or otherwise, upon notification to affected parties as required by the court."[263]

[253] Ray v. Porter, 464 F.2d 452 (6th Cir. 1972) (statute of limitations tolled as to defendant servicemember, but not as to defendant non-servicemember spouse; cause of action properly maintained against former and properly dismissed as to latter). *Accord* Card v. American Brands Corp., 401 F. Supp. 1186 (D.C.N.Y. 1975) (non-servicemember's loss of consortium barred); Wanner v. Glen Ellen Corp., 373 F. Supp. 983 (D.C. Vt. 1974) (loss of consortium claim barred even though derivative to servicemember's claims).

[254] 50 U.S.C. app. § 526(a) (LEXIS 2006).

[255] Miller v. United States, 803 F.Supp. 1120 (E. D. Va. 1992).

[256] *See, e.g., In re* a Child Whose First Name is Baby Girl, 615 N.Y.S. 2d 800, 801 (N.Y. App. Div. 1994) ("father failed to do all that he could to establish a parental relationship within the six months immediately preceding the child's placement for adoption").

[257] Dellape v. Murray, 651 A. 2d 638 (Pa. Commw. Ct. 1994).

[258] *See, e.g.*, Wells v. Brown, 9 Vet. App. 293 (1996); Carr v. United States, 422 F.2d 1007 (4th Cir. 1970) (no tolling where United States was substituted for servicemember as party to the suit).

[259] Min v. Avila, 991 S.W.2d 495 (Tex. App. 1999).

[260] Bowen v. United States, 49 Fed. Cl. 673, 676 (2001), *aff'd*, 292 F.3d 1383 (Fed. Cir. 2002)

[261] 50 U.S.C.S. app. § 511(2)(C) (LEXIS 2006).

[262] Mason v. Texaco, 862 F.2d 242, 244 (10th Cir. 1988).

[263] 50 U.S.C. app. § 583.

This section permits a court that has issued an interlocutory order under the Act to revoke, modify, or extend such an order on its own motion or otherwise. This section has relevance when read together with other sections that allow a court to grant certain relief and then allow the court to do things such as "in the interest of all parties." For example, section 531, which deals with eviction and distress, allows a court to grant a 90-day stay of eviction proceedings "unless in the opinion of the court, justice and equity require a longer or shorter period of time."[264] Thus, the court could issue whatever interlocutory orders its rules of procedure allowed in such a proceeding if it found that such an order would be equitable for all the parties involved.

XI. Garnishment of Pay

Section 5220a, title 5, United States Code,[265] outlines how a judgment creditor may garnish pay from a federal employee. In the case of servicemembers, although their pay is subject to garnishment, it is possible for them to interpose two defenses. First, the creditor must "be in compliance with the procedural requirements of the Servicemembers Civil Relief Act."[266] Second, the servicemember may be able to show that there was an "absence . . . from an appearance in a judicial proceeding resulting from the exigencies of military duty.[267]

The Department of Defense (DoD) implements this statute through *DoD Directive. 1344.9*[268] and *DoD Instruction 1344.12.*[269] In fact, the DoD outlines the requirements for processing "debt complaints"[270] as well as requests to establish an involuntary allotment.[271] In accordance with the statutory mandate, the DoD will not authorize an involuntary allotment if there is a lack of compliance with the SCRA.[272] As to what these procedural requirements are, neither the statute nor the implementing instruction are clear. One can surmise, however, that the most likely procedures a creditor must comply with are those related to default judgments.[273] A creditor, that is, must comply with the default rules in order to obtain an involuntary allotment against a servicemember.[274]

An involuntary allotment will not be established if military exigencies have hindered the defendant-servicemember. "Exigencies of military duty" are defined as follows:

[264] *Id.* § 531(b)(1)(A).
[265] 5 U.S.C.S. § 5220a (LEXIS 2006).
[266] *Id.* § 5220a(k)(2)(A).
[267] *Id.* § 5220a(k)(2)(B).
[268] DOD DIR. 1344.9, *supra* note 235.
[269] DOD INSTR. 1344.12, *supra* note 236.
[270] *Id.* para. 6.1.
[271] *Id.* para. 6.2.
[272] *Id.* para. 6.2.2.5.3.1.
[273] *See* Major Howard McGillan, *Defenses to Involuntary Allotments for Creditor Judgments—Implementing the Hatch Act Reform Amendments*, ARMY LAW., Jan. 1995, at 68.
[274] *See supra* paras. 3-2 and 3-4

> A military assignment or mission-essential duty that, because of its urgency, importance, duration, location, or isolation, necessitates the absence of a member of the Military Services from appearance at a judicial proceeding or prevents the member from being able to respond to a notice of application for an involuntary allotment. Exigency of military duty is normally presumed during periods of war, national emergency, or when the member is deployed.[275]

XII. Practical Considerations

Servicemembers and their attorneys should be aware of several additional practical consequences in addition to the consequences and technical application discussed thus far. Foremost among these is consideration about whether s/he should take advantage of the Act. There may be times when defending, rather than staying, may be a better option. While the statute of limitations may be tolled, there are times when the servicemember will be better off to bring the suit as soon as possible and avoid the risk that it will be defeated on a claim of laches.

Next, state law should be consulted for at least three reasons. First, as a very basic matter, there is a need to make sure that other procedural aspects of the litigation have been met. For example, has there been effective service? Next, many states have adopted legislation that is similar, if not the same as, the SCRA. Although a seemingly needless redundancy, this was often done as a way to insure that Guardsmen, left unprotected by the SSCRA and SCRA, were given some form of relief. Regardless, these state protections may also protect other reserve and active component members. In any event, despite the SCRA's long history and despite its place as a cornerstone of veterans' legislation, there are times when a court will be more easily persuaded when it is shown that the action is valid as a matter of state law. Finally, there are times when the state SCRA-like provisions will actually extend protections.[276]

[275] DOD DIR. 1344.9, *supra* note 235, para. E2.1.4.

[276] *See, e.g.*, *In re* Marriage of Thompson, 832 P.2d 349 (1992) (although defendant fell outside of SSCRA default protections, application of state provision led to relief from judgment); Bernhardt v. Alden Café, 864 A.2d 421, 422 (2005) ("We hold that default should have been set vacated under the New Jersey Soldiers' and Sailors' Civil Relief Act"). Jusino v. New York City Hous. Auth., 691 N.Y.S.2d 12, 17 (N.Y. App. Div. 1999) (New York stay provisions held to cover "an infant who is in the care of a parent whose military duty causes the infant to be unable to 'represent his interest'").

Chapter 4

Evictions, Leases, Installment Contracts, Mortgages, and Similar Protections

I. *Introduction*

Title III of the SCRA (50 U.S.C. §§ 531-537) provides for a number of similar benefits and protections. For example, it provides protection against eviction[1] and protection against repossession of property.[2] This chapter will examine the Title III protections and benefits as well as certain other related provisions.

II. *Extension of Benefits to Dependents*

All Title III protections are applicable to dependents[3] in their own right. The applicable section indicates that "[u]pon application to a court, a dependent of a servicemember is entitled to the protections of this title if the dependent's ability to comply with a lease, contract, bailment, or other obligation is materially affected by reason of the servicemember's military service."[4] Congress added this section's prede-

[1] 50 U.S.C.S. app. § 531 (LEXIS 2006).

[2] *Id.* app. § 532.

[3] It is worth remembering that the definition of "dependents" is broader than the spouse and children of the servicemember.

> The term "dependent," with respect to a servicemember, means (A) the servicemember's spouse; (B) the servicemember's child (as defined in section 101(4) of title 38, United States Code); or (C) an individual for whom the servicemember provided more than one-half of the individual's support for 180 days immediately preceding an application for relief under this Act.

Id. app. § 511(4).

[4] *Id.* app. § 538.

cessor in 1942 to avoid situations in which dependents suffered as a result of the servicemember's period of service.

Perhaps the most important thing to note about this provision is that the servicemember's military service must materially affect the dependent's ability to comply with the obligation in question.[5] Under the terms of this section, dependents of military personnel may apply to a court for the benefits of all the sections under Title III. If the court finds that the dependent's ability to comply with the terms of a contract or other obligation is materially affected by the military service of the person upon whom he or she is dependent, then the court is authorized to grant the dependent at least the same degree of relief to which the servicemember would be entitled.[6] At least one court has held that the benefit is available even for property acquired prior to marrying a servicemember.[7] Another has held that Title III protection against eviction[8] exists even after a marriage when the former spouse is still financially dependent on the servicemember.[9]

III. Eviction and Distress

The SCRA protects against the eviction of servicemembers:

> 50 U.S.C. app. § 531
>
> (a) Court—ordered eviction.
> - (1) In general. Except by court order, a landlord (or another person with paramount title) may not—
>   - (A) evict a servicemember, or the dependents of a servicemember, during a period of military service of the servicemember, from premises—
>   - (i) that are occupied or intended to be occupied primarily as a residence; and
>   - (ii) for which the monthly rent does not exceed $2,400, as adjusted under paragraph (2) for years after 2003; or
>   - (B) subject such premises to a distress during the period of military service.

[5] It is instructive to compare the current provision with the older one:

> Dependents of a person in military service shall be entitled to the benefits accorded to persons in military service under the provisions of this article upon application to a court therefore, unless in the opinion of the court the ability of such dependents to comply with the terms of the obligation, contract, lease, or bailment has not been materially impaired by reason of the military service of the person upon whom the applicants are dependent.

50 U.S.C. app. § 536 (2000).

[6] *See, e.g.*, Reid v. Margolis, 44 N.Y.S.2d 518 (1943); Pfeiffer v. McGarvey, 61 F. Supp. 570 (E.D. Pa. 1945).

[7] Tucson Telco & Fed. Credit Union v. Bowser, 451 P.2d 322 (Ariz. Ct. App. 1969).

[8] 50 U.S.C.S. app. § 531 (LEXIS 2006).

[9] Balconi v. Dvascas, 507 N.Y.S.2d 788 (1986).

(2) Housing price inflation adjustment.
   (A) For calendar years beginning with 2004, the amount in effect under paragraph (1)(A)(ii) shall be increased by the housing price inflation adjustment for the calendar year involved.
   (B) For purposes of this paragraph—
      (i) The housing price inflation adjustment for any calendar year is the percentage change (if any) by which—
         (I) the CPI housing component for November of the preceding calendar year, exceeds
         (II) the CPI housing component for November of 1984.
      (ii) The term "CPI housing component" means the index published by the Bureau of Labor Statistics of the Department of Labor known as the Consumer Price Index, All Urban Consumers, Rent of Primary Residence, U.S. City Average.

(3) Publication of housing price inflation adjustment. The Secretary of Defense shall cause to be published in the Federal Register each year the amount in effect under paragraph (1)(A)(ii) for that year following the housing price inflation adjustment for that year pursuant to paragraph (2). Such publication shall be made for a year not later than 60 days after such adjustment is made for that year.

(b) Stay of execution.
   (1) Court authority. Upon an application for eviction or distress with respect to premises covered by this section, the court may on its own motion and shall, if a request is made by or on behalf of a servicemember whose ability to pay the agreed rent is materially affected by military service—
      (A) stay the proceedings for a period of 90 days, unless in the opinion of the court, justice and equity require a longer or shorter period of time; or
      (B) adjust the obligation under the lease to preserve the interests of all parties.
   (2) Relief to landlord. If a stay is granted under paragraph (1), the court may grant to the landlord (or other person with paramount title) such relief as equity may require.

(c) Penalties.
   (1) Misdemeanor. Except as provided in subsection (a), a person who knowingly takes part in an eviction or distress described in subsection (a), or who knowingly attempts to do so, shall be fined as provided in title 18, United States Code, or imprisoned for not more than one year, or both.
   (2) Preservation of other remedies and rights. The remedies and rights provided under this section are in addition to and do not preclude any remedy for wrongful conversion (or wrongful eviction) otherwise available under the law to the person claiming relief under this section, including any award for consequential and punitive damages.

(d) Rent allotment from pay of servicemember. To the extent required by a court order related to property which is the subject of a court action under this section, the Secretary concerned shall make an allotment from the pay of a servicemember to satisfy the terms of such order, except that any such allotment shall be subject to regulations prescribed by the Secretary concerned establishing the maximum amount of pay of servicemembers that may be allotted under this subsection.

(e) Limitation of applicability. Section 202 [50 U.S.C. app. § 522] is not applicable to this section.[10]

This section protects servicemembers and their dependents from eviction for non-payment of rent. It does not preclude eviction, but it does set up the process through which that remedy must pass. Notwithstanding any process that might be permitted under state law, the landlord must obtain a court order. Upon the servicemember's or family member's request and upon a showing that there is material effect, the court must stay the proceeding for roughly ninety days.[11] Additionally, the court may "adjust the obligation under the lease to preserve the interests of all parties"[12] and if it grants a stay it "may grant to the landlord (or other person with paramount title) such relief as equity may require."[13]

The SCRA does not define "eviction" or "distress," but "[t]here is nothing to indicate that the terms . . . are used to imply anything other than the usually and commonly accepted meaning[s].[14] "Eviction," then, simply enough, "is dispossession of a tenant by a landlord."[15]

As of January 2006, servicemembers were protected if the rent did not exceed $2615.16. As originally enacted, the rent could not exceed $2400.00 in order for the protection to apply.[16]

The $2615.16 figure represents the annual adjustment for inflation[17] as published

[10] 50 U.S.C. app. § 531.

[11] The SCRA is a bit open-ended on this point indicating that the court shall "stay the proceedings for a period of 90 days, unless in the opinion of the court, justice and equity require a longer or shorter period of time." *Id.* app. § 531(b)(1)(A).

[12] *Id.* app. § 531(b)(1)(B).

[13] *Id.* app. § 531(b)(2). It is not entirely clear how these last two provisions are meant to work. Obviously, the court might adjust the obligation so that the landlord is not at some complete loss. Perhaps if a mobilization were to be of short duration, the equitable relief might be for the servicemember/tenant to pay the difference off over a period of time when s/he returns from active duty. In one case, the court stayed the eviction. During the period of the eviction, the servicemember did not pay any rent, but offered to pay the fourth month's rent; that is, the rent due for the month following the stay. The court accepted this offer rather than grant the landlord the eviction, but ordered that the rent for the period of the stay was still due and owing. *See* Jonda Realty Corp. v. Marabotto, 34 N.Y.S.2d 301 (Sup. Ct. 1942).

[14] Lesher v. Louisville Gas & Elec. Co., 49 F. Supp. 88, 89 (W.D. Ky. 1943).

[15] *Id.*

[16] 50 U.S.C. app. § 531(a)(1)(A)(ii).

[17] *Id.* app. § 531(a)(2)(A).

annually[18] in the Federal Register.[19] This annual increase will obviously warrant attention.

Section 531 provides criminal sanctions against those who knowingly take part in the eviction or attempted eviction of the spouse, children, or other dependents of a servicemember from any premises occupied as a dwelling and rented for less than $2615.16.[20] This sanction is in addition to "other rights and remedies" that may be available to the servicemember.[21] In fact, a violation of this section may also support an action for damages for wrongful eviction to include an award of punitive damages.[22]

Courts have required that a landlord-tenant relationship exist as this section contemplates a disturbance of that relationship. The extension of these provisions beyond landlords to include "other person[s] with paramount title"[23] is interesting. It evinces Congress's perceived need "to eliminate the conflict between courts regarding the relationship required to invoke the eviction protections of this section."[24] In doing so, Congress meant to adopt the more liberal, if not realistic, approach taken in *Clinton Cotton Mills v. United States*.[25] In that case, the servicemember, Charles Thomas, had worked for Clinton Cotton Mills and had rented company housing from the mill prior to his induction into the armed forces. The trial court convicted the defendant cotton mill for the misdemeanor crime of wrongful eviction, when it evicted Thomas's family from company housing following the termination of his employment and induction.[26] Following the first eviction, the servicemember's family began residing at the home of another company employee, Roy Ramsey, who rented company housing from the mill. This meant that Ramsey was technically the Thomas's' landlord. The company was held liable for this second count of wrongful eviction when it threatened to evict Ramsey if the Thomases did not leave. The court stated that "a tenant can be evicted only by his landlord, but this is not true when a tenant is deprived of possession by one who has title paramount to the tenant's immediate landlord . . ."[27] Congress highlighted its choice of outcome by contrasting the result in *Clinton* to that in

[18] *Id.* app. § 531(a)(3).

[19] For 2006, *see* Publication of Housing Price Inflation Adjustment Under 50 U.S.C. app. § 531, 71 Fed. Reg. 2530 (Jan. 17, 2006). In 2005, the amount was $2534.32. *See* Publication of Housing Price Inflation Adjustment Under 50 U.S.C. app. § 531, 701 Fed. Reg. 2395 (Jan. 13, 2005). In 2004, shortly after the SCRA's adoption, the amount was $2465.00. *See* Publication of Housing Price Inflation Adjustment Under Public Law 108-189, Section 301, Fed. Reg. 1281 (Jan. 8, 2004).

[20] 50 U.S.C. app. § 531(c)(1).

[21] *Id.* app. § 531(c)(2).

[22] *See, e.g.*, Prather v. Clover Spinning Mills, Inc., 54 S.E.2d 529, 535 (1949)("Defendants' failure to follow the Federal statute, with knowledge of plaintiff's dependence upon her son in the service, to which she testified, fully justified the verdict for punitive damages").

[23] 50 U.S.C. app. § 531(a)(1).

[24] H.R. REP. NO.108-81, at 40 (2003).

[25] 164 F.2d 173 (4th Cir. 1947).

[26] *Id.* at 174-5.

[27] *Id.* at 176.

Arkless v. Kilstein.[28] In *Arkless*, the district court had held that "the Act refers to, in its commonly accepted legal interpretation, to a dispossession of a tenant by a landlord, and not to any disturbance of the tenant's right to possession and quiet enjoyment of the premises by a third party."[29]

Section 531(d) provides for the possibility that allotments may be taken from a servicemember's pay.[30] This requires secretarial implementation and currently there is no procedure authorized.[31]

IV. Residential Leases

In addition to the protections against evictions,[32] the SCRA allows servicemembers to terminate residential leases. In fact, the SCRA, in contrast to the SSCRA, has expanded this gamut of protections and added similar protections for servicemembers who lease automobiles. Practitioners will undoubtedly conclude that this section must be read with a degree of care. The portions which deal with residential leases and those concerning automobile leases are similar, but they operate under different timelines. Thus, care must be taken to avoid using or advocating from the wrong timeline.

In any event, the entire section is as follows:

50 U.S.C. app. § 535

(a) Termination by lessee.
  (1) In general. The lessee on a lease described in subsection (b) may, at the lessee's option, terminate the lease at any time after—
    (A) the lessee's entry into military service; or
    (B) the date of the lessee's military orders described in paragraph (1)(B) or (2)(B) of subsection (b), as the case may be.
  (2) Joint leases. A lessee's termination of a lease pursuant to this subsection shall terminate any obligation a dependent of the lessee may have under the lease.
(b) Covered leases. This section applies to the following leases:
  (1) Leases of premises. A lease of premises occupied, or intended to be occupied, by a servicemember or a servicemember's dependents for a residential, professional, business, agricultural, or similar purpose if—
    (A) the lease is executed by or on behalf of a person who thereafter and during the term of the lease enters military service; or
    (B) the servicemember, while in military service, executes the lease and thereafter receives military orders for a change of permanent station or to deploy with a military unit, or as an individual in support of a military operation, for a period of not less than 90 days.

[28] 61 F. Supp. 886 (E.D. Pa. 1944). *See also* H.R. REP. NO.108-81, at 40.
[29] *Arkless*, 61 F. Supp. at 888.
[30] 50 U.S.C. app. § 531(d).
[31] U.S. DEP'T OF DEFENSE, REG. 7000.14-R, FINANCIAL MANAGEMENT REGULATION vol. 7A, ch. 50 (July 2005).
[32] *See* 50 U.S.C. app. § 531. *See also supra* para. 4-3.

(2) Leases of motor vehicles. A lease of a motor vehicle used, or intended to be used, by a servicemember or a servicemember's dependents for personal or business transportation if—
  (A) the lease is executed by or on behalf of a person who thereafter and during the term of the lease enters military service under a call or order specifying a period of not less than 180 days (or who enters military service under a call or order specifying a period of 180 days or less and who, without a break in service, receives orders extending the period of military service to a period of not less than 180 days); or
  (B) the servicemember, while in military service, executes the lease and thereafter receives military orders—
    (i) for a change of permanent station—
      (I) from a location in the continental United States to a location outside the continental United States; or
      (II) from a location in a State outside the continental United States to any location outside that State; or
    (ii) to deploy with a military unit, or as an individual in support of a military operation, for a period of not less than 180 days.

(c) Manner of termination.
  (1) In general. Termination of a lease under subsection (a) is made—
    (A) by delivery by the lessee of written notice of such termination, and a copy of the servicemember's military orders, to the lessor (or the lessor's grantee), or to the lessor's agent (or the agent's grantee); and
    (B) in the case of a lease of a motor vehicle, by return of the motor vehicle by the lessee to the lessor (or the lessor's grantee), or to the lessor's agent (or the agent's grantee), not later than 15 days after the date of the delivery of written notice under subparagraph (A).
  (2) Delivery of notice. Delivery of notice under paragraph (1)(A) may be accomplished—
    (A) by hand delivery;
    (B) by private business carrier; or
    (C) by placing the written notice in an envelope with sufficient postage and with return receipt requested, and addressed as designated by the lessor (or the lessor's grantee) or to the lessor's agent (or the agent's grantee), and depositing the written notice in the United States mails.

(d) Effective date of lease termination.
  (1) Lease of premises. In the case of a lease described in subsection (b)(1) that provides for monthly payment of rent, termination of the lease under subsection (a) is effective 30 days after the first date on which the next rental payment is due and payable after the date on which the notice under subsection (c) is delivered. In the case of any other lease described in subsection (b)(1), termination of the lease under subsection (a) is effective on the last day of the month following the month in which the notice is delivered.

(2) Lease of motor vehicles. In the case of a lease described in subsection (b)(2), termination of the lease under subsection (a) is effective on the day on which the requirements of subsection (c) are met for such termination.

(e) Arrearages and other obligations and liabilities. Rents or lease amounts unpaid for the period preceding the effective date of the lease termination shall be paid on a prorated basis. In the case of the lease of a motor vehicle, the lessor may not impose an early termination charge, but any taxes, summonses, and title and registration fees and any other obligation and liability of the lessee in accordance with the terms of the lease, including reasonable charges to the lessee for excess wear, use and mileage, that are due and unpaid at the time of termination of the lease shall be paid by the lessee.

(f) Rent paid in advance. Rents or lease amounts paid in advance for a period after the effective date of the termination of the lease shall be refunded to the lessee by the lessor (or the lessor's assignee or the assignee's agent) within 30 days of the effective date of the termination of the lease.

(g) Relief to lessor. Upon application by the lessor to a court before the termination date provided in the written notice, relief granted by this section to a servicemember may be modified as justice and equity require.

(h) Penalties.

(1) Misdemeanor. Any person who knowingly seizes, holds, or detains the personal effects, security deposit, or other property of a servicemember or a servicemember's dependent who lawfully terminates a lease covered by this section, or who knowingly interferes with the removal of such property from premises covered by such lease, for the purpose of subjecting or attempting to subject any of such property to a claim for rent accruing subsequent to the date of termination of such lease, or attempts to do so, shall be fined as provided in title 18, United States Code, or imprisoned for not more than one year, or both.

(2) Preservation of other remedies. The remedy and rights provided under this section are in addition to and do not preclude any remedy for wrongful conversion otherwise available under law to the person claiming relief under this section, including any award for consequential or punitive damages.

(i) Definitions.

(1) Military orders. The term "military orders," with respect to a servicemember, means official military orders, or any notification, certification, or verification from the servicemember's commanding officer, with respect to the servicemember's current or future military duty status.

(2) CONUS. The term "continental United States" means the 48 contiguous States and the District of Columbia.[33]

[33] 50 U.S.C. app. § 535.

This section of the Act differs from the section concerning evictions.[34] It provides a method by which the servicemember-lessee rather than the lessor, may terminate a lease. Its scope is not limited by either the amount of the agreed rent or the nature of the premises. In further contrast, this section does not require that the lessee's ability to perform be materially affected by his/her military service.

Servicemembers who come to active duty from the reserve components or those who join the armed forces[35] are allowed to terminate their "residential, professional, business, [or] agricultural"[36] leases. They must do this in writing, however.[37] As a concession to the lessor, the termination "is effective 30 days after the first date on which the next rental payment is due and payable"[38] and after the notice has been delivered.[39] For example, in the case of a month-to-month rental, the termination becomes effective 30 days after the first date on which the next rental payment is due subsequent to the date when the notice of termination is delivered. If the rent is due on the first day of each month, and notice is mailed on 1 August, then "the next rental payment is due and payable" on 1 September. Thirty days after that date would be 1 October.

There is also the possibility that a lessor may obtain equitable relief,[40] the lessor may, during the period from his/her receipt of notice to the effective date of termination, petition the appropriate court for relief from the lease termination. Landlords may petition the court on grounds of "undue hardship" or countervailing equitable consideration or for an "equitable offset" for lease termination. Such an "equitable offset" would most likely be granted in commercial or professional lease terminations. "Equitable offset" could include lost rent, realty fees for re-rental, deprecation in rental value of premises because of tenant-requested fixtures, and attorney fees and costs.[41] In addition, if the servicemember requires the lessor to modify the property and subsequently terminates the lease, the lessor may charge the lessee for the alterations.[42] This occurs only if the lessee knew of the impending call to active duty at the time the lessee requested the modifications.[43]

Although there is a possibility that equity will require relief to the lessor, the servicemember's ability to terminate a lease is a clearly defined protection. Thus, "a

[34] *Id.* app. § 531. *See also supra* para. 4-3.
[35] 50 U.S.C. app. § 535(a)(1)(B).
[36] *Id.* app. § 535(b)(1).
[37] *Id.* app. § 535(c).
[38] *Id.* app. § 535(d)(1).
[39] *Id.*
[40] *Id.* app. § 535(g).
[41] Omega Indus. v. Raffaele, 894 F. Supp. 1425, 1430 (D. Nev., 1995) ("For example, if a military person who knows that he or she will soon be invoking [50 U.S.C. app. § 535] to terminate an existing lease—wrongfully induces a lessor to make tenant improvements, a court may find that equity requires that an equitable remedy be granted in an amount equal to both the cost of those improvements and the monthly rental obligations of that military person").
[42] *Id.*
[43] *Id.*

court in equity must exercise extreme caution in withholding the protection."[44] The law makes it clear that prepaid rents, for instance, are to be returned to the lessee 30 days after "the effective date of termination."[45] As with other Title III protections, violations can be criminally sanctioned[46] and damages from a lessor's actions, to include punitive damages, can also be obtained.[47]

Perhaps the most important thing to note about this provision is that it is applicable when a servicemember is transferred from one duty location to another or when ordered to deploy "for a period of not less than 90 days."[48] In the past, legal assistance practitioners have been concerned to see that members of their command execute leases with so called "military clauses." Leases with these provisions allow for the early termination of a lease when a servicemember is notified of a transfer to a new duty assignment. Even though a servicemember would be well advised to still include such a clause, the SCRA obviates the need to contract for this relief.

Another very important aspect of the protection concerns the fact that it applies to joint leases.[49] This provision is important for those servicemembers who deploy with a unit and who leave a spouse behind who wishes to reside somewhere other than near the servicemember's duty station. That spouse's obligation is terminated along with that of the servicemember's.[50]

Taking this a step further, it should be noted as well that one would normally think of a servicemember's co-tenant spouse as the person with a need to terminate the lease. The law, as it turns out, is a bit broader allowing for the termination by not just a spouse, but by any dependent who has signed the lease with the servicemember.[51] A "dependent" includes a spouse, but also "an individual for whom the servicemember provided more than one-half of the individual's support for 180 days immediately preceding an application for relief."[52] One can certainly imagine situations involving an elderly parent who needs to terminate a lease while the servicemember is deployed.

V. *Automobile Leases*

The SCRA's automobile provisions[53] truly bring the law into the modern era. Although the scheme is parallel to the portion of the law concerning residential leases, practitioners should note that the period of active duty is longer if the protections are to be effective. While residential leases may be terminated when a servicemember enters

[44] *Id.* at 1434.
[45] 50 U.S,C. app. § 535(f).
[46] *Id.* app. § 535(h)(1).
[47] *Id.* app. § 535(h)(2).
[48] *Id.* app. § 535(b)(1)(B).
[49] *Id.* app. § 535(a)(2).
[50] *Id.*
[51] *Id.*
[52] *Id.* app. § 511(4).
[53] *Id.* app. § 535(b)(2).

active duty for a period of 90 days,[54] an automobile lease may only be terminated after 180 days.[55]

Servicemembers may also terminate their automobile leases when they receive orders for a permanent change of station (PCS) from a posting in the continental United States to another location outside the continental United States.[56] If they are stationed outside the continental United States, but in a United States territory or state, they may terminate the lease if they are transferred to the continental United States or to another state or territory outside the continental United States.[57] Finally, servicemembers who are not subject to a PCS, but who "deploy with a military unit, or as an individual in support of a military operation,"[58] may also seek relief if the deployment is for at least 180 days.[59]

VI. Installment Contracts

Under Section 532, the SCRA protects servicemembers who enter into installment contracts prior to entry on active duty:

50 U.S.C. app. § 532

(a) Protection upon breach of contract.
   (1) Protection after entering military service. After a servicemember enters military service, a contract by the servicemember for—
      (A) the purchase of real or personal property (including a motor vehicle); or
      (B) the lease or bailment of such property, may not be rescinded or terminated for a breach of terms of the contract occurring before or during that person's military service, nor may the property be repossessed for such breach without a court order.
   (2) Applicability. This section applies only to a contract for which a deposit or installment has been paid by the servicemember before the servicemember enters military service.
(b) Penalties.
   (1) Misdemeanor. A person who knowingly resumes possession of property in violation of subsection (a), or in violation of section 107 of this Act [50 U.S.C. app. § 517], or who knowingly attempts to do so, shall be fined as provided in title 18, United States Code, or imprisoned for not more than one year, or both.
   (2) Preservation of other remedies and rights. The remedies and rights provided under this section are in addition to and do not preclude any

[54] *Id.* app. § 535(b)(1)(B).
[55] *Id.* app. § 535(b)(2)(A).
[56] *Id.* app. § 535(b)(2)(B)(i)(I).
[57] *Id.* app. § 535(b)(2)(B)(i)(II).
[58] *Id.* app. § 535(b)(2)(B)(ii).
[59] *Id.*

remedy for wrongful conversion otherwise available under law to the person claiming relief under this section, including any award for consequential and punitive damages.

(c) Authority of court. In a hearing based on this section, the court—

(1) may order repayment to the servicemember of all or part of the prior installments or deposits as a condition of terminating the contract and resuming possession of the property;

(2) may, on its own motion, and shall on application by a servicemember when the servicemember's ability to comply with the contract is materially affected by military service, stay the proceedings for a period of time as, in the opinion of the court, justice and equity require; or

(3) may make other disposition as is equitable to preserve the interests of all parties.[60]

A. Installment Contract Basics

The first and foremost protection offered by this section is that repossession of either real or personal property, being purchased under an installment contract, may not be repossessed from a defaulting servicemember unless there is a court order.[61] The vendor is, in other words, prohibited from exercising any right or option under the contract to rescind or terminate the contract, to resume possession of the property for nonpayment of any installment due, or to breach the terms, except by action in a court of competent jurisdiction. Again, this must be a contract that existed prior to the servicemember's entry on active duty. Contracts entered into following entry on active duty are not covered.[62] It is immaterial, however, whether the nonpayment or other breach occurs prior to or during the period of military service. If the contract was entered into prior to military service and if an installment or deposit has been made, then the creditor must apply to a court before seeking to repossess or otherwise dispose of the property.[63]

A knowing violation of this provision of the SCRA can result in a misdemeanor conviction.[64] Property repossessed without benefit of the requisite court action will subject the creditor to a suit for wrongful conversion.[65]

There are three other remedies available under section 532. First, when one of these matters comes before the court, the court can on its own decide to stay the pro-

[60] *Id.* app. § 532.

[61] *Id.* app. § 532(a)(1)((b). *See, e.g.*, Hanson v. Crown Toyota Motors, Inc., 572 P.2d 380 (Utah, 1977).

[62] 50 U.S.C. app. § 532(a)(2). *See, e.g.*, Jim's Trailer Sales, Inc. v. Shutok, 153 F. Supp. 274 (W.D. Pa. 1957); Charles H. Jenkins & Co., Inc. v. Lewis, 130 S.E.2d 49 (1963).

[63] *See, e.g.*, Hampton v. Commercial Credit Corp., 176 P.2d 270 (1946).

[64] 50 U.S.C. app. § 532(b)(1). Other remedies, such as consequential and punitive damages, are also available. *Id.* app. § 532(b)(2).

[65] *See Hanson.*, 572 P.2d 380; Pac. Fin. Corp. v. Gilkerson, 217 S.W.2d 440 (Tex. Civ. App. 1949); Application of Aber, 40 N.Y.S.2d 48 (Sup. Ct. 1942). *See also Hampton*, 176 P.2d 270 (lack of evidence, but "exemplary damages" a consideration under former SSCRA).

ceeding "for a period of time, as in the opinion of the court, justice and equity require."[66] The court must stay the proceeding if the servicemember makes a request for the stay and if there is a showing that the servicemember's military service has materially affected the servicemember's ability to meet the obligation.[67] The court can also "make other disposition as is equitable to preserve the interests of all parties."[68] Third, if the court concludes that the property is subject to repossession, it may also "order repayment to the servicemember of all or part of the prior installments or deposits."[69]

B. Material Effect

As to the installment provision, it is most important to note that material effect is only a requirement when the court looks to stay the matter pending final resolution. Under the prior law, it was possible to argue that material effect was a necessary element if the servicemember were to have the contract terminated and the installments repaid.[70]

[66] *Id.* app. § 532(c)(2).

[67] *Id.*

[68] *Id.* app. § 532(c)(3).

[69] *Id.* app. 532(c)(1). *See also id.* app. § 534 (appraisal and payment of equity in repossessed property). There are few cases that examine or otherwise provide guidance on how a court might come to this equitable balance. In one case, nonetheless, where the court found that a servicemember's ability to comply had been materially affected by his military service, but any delay in enforcement would impose an "unnecessary, unexpected and unjustifiable hardship" on the creditor, "without bringing any benefit to" the servicemember, the court refused to grant a stay and resorted to its equitable powers to resolve the dilemma. Assocs. Discount Corp. v. Armstrong, 33 N.Y.S.2d 36, 38 (Rochester City Ct. 1942). Because the value of the security exceeded the amount due under the contract, the property was ordered sold, thereby terminating the servicemember's liability while the creditor received the balance due on the contract. *Id.* at 38-9. In another case in which the security for the obligation would have been destroyed or so diminished in value as to render it useless, the court ordered it sold and the proceeds divided proportionately. Holtzman's Furniture Store v. Schrapf, 39 So.2d 450, (La. App., 1949).

[70] *See* 50 app. § 532(c)(2). The former provision, which lumped the three remedies together, was as follows:

> Upon the hearing of such action the court may order the repayment of prior installments or deposits or any part thereof, as a condition of terminating the contract and resuming possession of the property, or may, in its discretion, on its own motion, and shall, on application to it by such person in military service or some person on his behalf, order a stay of proceedings as provided in this Act unless, in the opinion of the court, the ability of the defendant to comply with the terms of the contract is not materially affected by reason of such service; or it may make such other disposition of the case as may be equitable to conserve the interest of all parties.

50 U.S.C. app. § 531(3) (2000). Congress, in adopting the SCRA, has obviously enumerated the provisions and distinctly separated the three remedies.

There is also better logic to the notion that material effect is an implicit element if the court considers adjusting the equities.[71] In fact, under the prior law, some courts read this requirement into the statute[72] while others would not.[73]

That being said, the question becomes one of what constitutes material effect when that issue is properly before the court. In determining whether military service materially affects a servicemember's ability to meet his/her obligations, the court may compare his/her financial condition prior to entry on active duty with his/her condition while in military service.[74] Another factor that courts have considered is when the default or noncompliance by the servicemember began. When a pattern of noncompliance was begun long before the debtor's induction into the service, it can support a conclusion that military service was not the cause of the debtor's inability to meet the obligation.[75] Consequently, the servicemember seeking relief under this section must show hardship or material effect before he/she is entitled to protection under this section of the Act.

C. View to Purchase

Under the prior law the statute on installment contracts indicated that the protections and benefits were limited to those situations involving "a contract for the purchase of real or personal property, or of lease or bailment with a view to purchase of such property."[76] It should not go unnoted that the SCRA does not contain this language. As the House Committee on Veterans' Affairs explained, this was meant "to expand the section's protections to non-purchase leases, including leases for automobiles, business or professional equipment, farm equipment and other similar property."[77]

VII. *Mortgages*

The SCRA has provisions which affect mortgage foreclosures. The benefits, protections, and procedures are similar to others found in Title III. They are particularly similar to those involving installment contracts. The mortgage provision, however, is specifically designed to protect servicemembers against foreclosure of mortgages and other security interests. Although both are applicable to real or personal property trans-

[71] 50 U.S.C. app. § 532(c)(3).

[72] In one case involving the purchase of furniture, the court noted that "the . . . family now receives but a few dollars less than the gross earnings of defendant before his enlistment." *Holtzman's Furniture Store*, 39 So.2d at 455 (La. App., 1949). In deference to the vendor, the court likewise noted that "[n]o one will doubt for a moment that modern furniture does not improve with usage, and should the plaintiff herein be met with a stay order, there is no question that disadvantage would result." *Id. See also* Reese v. Bacon, 176 S.W.2d 971 (Tex. App., 1943).

[73] Hanson v. Crown Toyota Motors, Inc., 572 P.2d 380 (Utah, 1977).

[74] *See, e.g.*, Harvey v. Home Owners' Loan Corp., 67 N.Y.S.2d 586 (1946).

[75] *See* Creamer v. Ansoplano, 52 N.Y.S.2d 862 (Sup. Ct. 1945); *Reese*, 176 S.W.2d 971.

[76] 50 U.S.C. app. § 531(1) (2000).

[77] H.R. Rep. No.108-81, at 40 (2003).

actions, the installment contract provision does not require a security interest in the property. Given their similarity, decisions rendered under one provision may find utility under either. In any event, the mortgage provision is as follows:

50 U.S.C. app. § 533

(a) Mortgage as security. This section applies only to an obligation on real or personal property owned by a servicemember that—
   (1) originated before the period of the servicemember's military service and for which the servicemember is still obligated; and
   (2) is secured by a mortgage, trust deed, or other security in the nature of a mortgage.

(b) Stay of proceedings and adjustment of obligation. In an action filed during, or within 90 days after, a servicemember's period of military service to enforce an obligation described in subsection (a), the court may after a hearing and on its own motion and shall upon application by a servicemember when the servicemember's ability to comply with the obligation is materially affected by military service—
   (1) stay the proceedings for a period of time as justice and equity require, or
   (2) adjust the obligation to preserve the interests of all parties.

(c) Sale or foreclosure. A sale, foreclosure, or seizure of property for a breach of an obligation described in subsection (a) shall not be valid if made during, or within 90 days after, the period of the servicemember's military service except—
   (1) upon a court order granted before such sale, foreclosure, or seizure with a return made and approved by the court; or
   (2) if made pursuant to an agreement as provided in section 107 [50 U.S.C. app. § 517.]

(d) Penalties.
   (1) Misdemeanor. A person who knowingly makes or causes to be made a sale, foreclosure, or seizure of property that is prohibited by subsection (c), or who knowingly attempts to do so, shall be fined as provided in title 18, United States Code, or imprisoned for not more than one year, or both.
   (2) Preservation of other remedies. The remedies and rights provided under this section are in addition to and do not preclude any remedy for wrongful conversion otherwise available under law to the person claiming relief under this section, including consequential and punitive damages.[78]

[78] 50 U.S.C.S. app. § 533 (LEXIS 2006). Section 517, referenced in section 533, concerns waivers of SCRA protections that servicemembers may execute once they are entitled to those protections. *See id.* app. § 517. *See also supra* para. 2-5.

A. Mortgage Foreclosure Basics

This section applies to purchases of real or personal property that a servicemember makes prior to entry on active duty that are secured by a mortgage or trust deed.[79] If a servicemember breaches the obligation, a sale, foreclosure, or repossession action is not valid unless there is a court order or a waiver from the servicemember.[80] This protection is in addition to any state protection or requirement and extends ninety days beyond the servicemember's period of service.[81] Those who violate the provision could suffer a federal misdemeanor conviction[82] as well as a civil judgment for punitive damages and the like.[83] Of central importance, however, is a provision calling for a stay. A court can grant this relief on its own motion, but it must take action at the request of a servicemember following a showing of material effect.[84] Finally, there is a provision which allows a court to make an equitable adjustment.[85]

B. Ownership

The Act requires the servicemember (or his/her dependent)[86] to have "owned"[87] the mortgaged property prior to his/her entry upon active duty, continuing up to the time relief is sought from the court. Several questions relating to the nature of the ownership required to bring an obligation within the Act's coverage have been litigated.

Generally, the courts have interpreted the word "owned" to mean equitable and legal interests in property. This was the usage given under the Act of 1918[88] and the same meaning was applied to the SSCRA.[89] While the weight of authority supports this proposition, difficulties arise when innocent third parties who are purchasers for value without notice are involved. In these instances, the courts avoid exercising their equitable powers in favor of the servicemember by stating that "equitable" title must be recorded.[90]

C. Material Effect

In order for the court to stay or adjust the obligation, there must be a showing that the servicemember's military service materially affects his/her "ability to comply with the obligation."[91]

A mortgagee bringing a foreclosure action will provide the court with proof of the existence and the extent of the mortgage debt upon which suit is instituted and the date of default in payment. If favorable to him/her the mortgagee will often present the mortgagor's pre-service payment record. This is done when the record demonstrates pre-service default or a continuous pattern of tardy payments.[92]

Having determined that the servicemember "owned" the property, the trial court must then form an opinion on the ability of the servicemember to meet his/her financial obligations. That is, the court must determine whether military service has mate-

[79] 50 U.S.C. app. § 533(a).

[80] *Id.* app. § 533(c)(2). *See, e.g.*, Engstrom v. First Nat'l Bank of Eagle Lake, 47 F.3d 1459 (5th Cir. 1995).

[81] 50 U.S.C. app. § 533(c).

[82] *Id.* app. § 533 (d)(1).

[83] *Id.* app. § 533 (d)(2).

rially affected the servicemember's ability to discharge his/her pre-service responsibilities in the manner agreed upon. As one court has stated, "[t]he criterion, then, is a combination of two factors, *i.e.*, (1) whether the defendant's inability to comply results by reason of such military service, and (2) that such military service has materially affected the ability to comply."[93]

To secure relief, the servicemember should provide the court with sufficient financial information on the material effect of military service.[94] Two pieces of financial information are always essential: pre-service income and in-service income. Pre-service income, out of which the agreed mortgage payments were previously paid on time,[95] is considered as a standard. Typically, in-service income must not only be smaller, but it must be insufficient to reasonably maintain the servicemember before a court will grant relief.[96] Proof of in-service income should include showing the amount of (1) military pay and allowances, (2) allotments to dependents, and (3) any other non-military income, even if earned by dependents. In-service income should be treated as a net amount, because proof of any additional expense caused by military service is proper. When material effect is found, the courts exercise their discretion in fashioning appropriate relief.[97]

[84] *Id.* app. § 533(b)(1).

[85] *Id.* app. § 533(b)(2).

[86] *Id.* app. § 538.

[87] *Id.* app. § 533(a).

[88] Morse v. Stober, 123 N.E. 780 (1919); Hoffman v. Charlestown Five Cent Savings Bank, 231 Mass. 324, 121 N.E. 15 (1918).

[89] Fourth Nat'l Bank in Wichita v. Hill, 314 P.2d 312 (1957) (equitable title not established); Twitchell v. Home Owners' Loan Corp., 122 P.2d 210 (1942) (equitable interest established and servicemember/son allowed to intervene in case involving foreclosure against his mother).

[90] *See, e.g.*, Godwin v. Gerling, 239 S.W.2d 352 (1951).

[91] 50 U.S.C. app. § 533(b).

[92] Franklin Soc. for Home-Bldg. & Sav. v. Flavin, 40 N.Y.S.2d 582 (1943), *aff'd*, 291 N.Y. 530, 50 N.E.2d 653 (1944).

[93] Hunt v. Jacobson, 33 N.Y.S.2d 661, 664 (Sup. Ct. 1942). *See generally* Karen H. Switzer, *Mortgage Defaults and the Soldiers' and Sailors' Civil Relief Act: Assigning the Burden of Proof When Applying the Material Effect Test*, 18 REAL EST. L.J. 171, 177-84 (1989).

[94] The Act does not state which party has the burden of proof. The Supreme Court in Boone v. Lightner, 319 U.S 561 (1943), ruled that the burden of going forward would be determined by the trial courts. In some cases, the servicemember was required to prove material effect. *See, e.g.*, Queens County Sav. Bank v. Thaler, 44 N.Y.S.2d 4 (Sup. Ct. 1943). In other cases the one bringing the action against a service member had the burden of proving lack of material effect. *See, e.g.*, Meyers v. Schmidt, 46 N.Y.S.2d 420 (County Ct.1944). In any event, the servicemember should be prepared to go forward with sufficient evidence to support his/her position.

[95] *Meyers*, 46 N.Y.S.2d at 423 ("promptness in the payment of a bill may indicate ability to pay, the failure to be prompt in the payment of bills does not necessarily indicate inability to pay").

[96] *See, e.g.*, Hempstead Bank v. Collier, 289 N.Y.S.2d 797, 799 (Sup. Ct. 1967) ("net earnings have not been materially affected by his military service and in fact may actually have been improved").

[97] *See, e.g.*, Brown Serv. Ins. Co. v. King, 24 So.2d 219 (1945).

D. Nature of Relief

In a mortgage foreclosure proceeding, the Act generally provides the servicemember with three types of relief, which, under proper circumstances, are as follows:

(1) A stay of the proceedings, or an extension of the maturity dates of his/her obligations by way of diminished payments;
(2) Where foreclosure judgment has already been ordered, a reopening or setting aside of the judgment in order that the reviewer may assert a defense;[98] and
(3) Where a sale has been had under a judgment of foreclosure, invocation of the statutory redemption period, extended by a period equal to his/her military service.[99]

The extent of the mortgagor's financial disability resulting from military service heavily influences a court's decision on the measure of relief to be granted. Courts attempt to make equitable disposition of individual cases on their particular facts, in an effort "to preserve the interests of all parties."[100] This effort frequently results in granting the mortgagor, in appropriate cases, some form of conditional relief.[101]

Conditional relief usually involves a stay of the foreclosure proceedings on condition that the mortgagor makes some partial periodic payment on the outstanding mortgage debt.[102] In its discretion, the court determines to which of the incidents of the debt the payment will be applied. Although 50 U.S.C. app. § 533 prescribes no priority of application, a pattern has emerged from the cases. Usually, payments are applied in the following order: current and accrued taxes; hazard insurance; interest on the debt; and principal. Arrearages and FHA mortgage insurance premiums have been inserted in the priority scale in various fashions. So also have the application of sums from casualty insurance recoveries, amounts held in escrow by the mortgagee, and property surpluses.[103] Sometimes, when a court has granted a stay and ordered partial payments, the court has also required the servicemember to make periodic sworn state-

[98] The case should be examined, in the event of a default judgment, to determine whether there was either a false affidavit or a failure to file an affidavit as is required by 50 U.S.C.S. app. § 521 (LEXIS 2006). Such a defect may affect the validity of the judgment obtained. Wilkin v. Shell Oil Co., 197 F.2d 42 (10th Cir. 1951)

[99] *See* 50 U.S.C. app. § 526. *See also* Illinois Nat'l Bank of Springfield v. Gwinn, 107 N.E.2d 764 (1952); Radich v. Bloomberg, 54 A.2d 249 (1947); Flagg v. Sun Inv. & Loan Corp., 373 P.2d 226 (Okla. 1962).

[100] 50 U.S.C. app. § 533(b)(2).

[101] A court's examination of the servicemember's true financial situation may be the only protection for the lender, even in cases where the soldier obtained a mortgage after commencing active service. *See* Bruce H. White and William L. Medford, *The Soldiers' and Sailors' Civil Relief Act-Are You Stayed from Obtaining Relief from the Automatic Stay?*, 18 AM. BANKR. INST. J. 23 (1999).

[102] *See, e.g.*, Fed. Nat'l Mortgage Ass'n v. Deziel, 136 F. Supp. 859.

[103] *See* Brown Serv. Ins. Co. v. King, 24 So.2d 219; R.R. Fed. Sav. & Loan Ass'n v. Morrison, 40 N.Y.S.2d 319 (Sup. Ct. 1943); Nassau Sav. & Loan Ass'n v. Ormond, 39 N.Y.S.2d 92.

ments of his/her financial condition either to the court or to the mortgagee.[104] Conditional stay orders occasionally grant a mortgagee the right to apply for an amended stay order if the mortgagor's ability to discharge his/her debt becomes less impaired.[105] Such an amendment is within the court's power as a matter within its equitable powers and its continuing jurisdiction over the case.

E. Timing of Court Order

Under the prior law, there was some confusion over a requirement for a court order prior to foreclosure and sale of mortgaged property. This stemmed from language indicating that the foreclosure was not to take place "unless upon an order previously granted by the court."[106] A New Jersey Court had held that any such order must have been granted prior to the servicemember's entry on active duty[107] while a New York court held that the order must have been granted prior to foreclosure; that is, not before the servicemember's entry on active duty.[108] This should no longer be an issue given the provision indicating that the "court order [be] granted *before* such sale, foreclosure, or seizure."[109]

VIII. *Appraisals Following Foreclosures and Repossession*

This section is designed to provide supplemental relief for all parties when an installment contract or other obligation for purchase of personal property has been stayed under other sections of the Act.

[104] New York Life Ins. Co. v. Litke, 41 N.Y.S.2d 526, *modified on other grounds*, 45 N.Y.S.2d 576.

[105] *See, e.g.*, O'Leary v. Horgan, 39 N.Y.S.2d 555 (1943).

[106] 50 U.S.C. app. § 532(3) (2000).

[107] Stability Bldg. & Loan Ass'n v. Liebowitz, 28 A.2d 653 (1942).

[108] Syracuse Sav. Bank v. Brown, 42 N.Y.S.2d 156 (Sup. Ct. 1943).

[109] 50 U.S.C.S. app. § 533(c)(1) (LEXIS 2006). Congress' statement on this point likewise renders this a moot point:

> Section 303(c) [50 U.S.C. app. § 533(c)] on mortgages and trust deeds removes the words "unless upon an order previously granted by the court"' and inserts the words "upon a court order granted before such sale, foreclosure, or seizure." Two courts construing the original language have disagreed as to when the order must have been previously granted. One court held that the order must have been granted prior to the servicemember's entry onto active duty. *Stability Building and Loan Ass'n* v. *Liebowitz*, 132 N.J. Eq. 477, 28 A. 2d 653 (1942). Another court held that the order must issue prior to foreclosure on the property rather than entry onto active duty. *Syracuse Savings Bank* v. *Brown*, 181 Misc. 999, 42 N.Y.S. 2d 156 (N.Y. Sup. Ct. 1943). The Committee believes the latter interpretation is the correct view, being more consistent with the provision's language, "In any proceedings commenced in any court during the period of military service. . . ."

H.R. Rep. No. 108-81, at 40 (2003).

50 U.S.C. app. § 534

(a) Appraisal of property. When a stay is granted pursuant to this Act in a proceeding to foreclose a mortgage on or to repossess personal property, or to rescind or terminate a contract for the purchase of personal property, the court may appoint three disinterested parties to appraise the property.

(b) Equity payment. Based on the appraisal, and if undue hardship to the servicemember's dependents will not result, the court may order that the amount of the servicemember's equity in the property be paid to the servicemember, or the servicemember's dependents, as a condition of foreclosing the mortgage, repossessing the property, or rescinding or terminating the contract.[110]

This section is applicable in cases where a stay has been granted under this Act in "[a[ny] proceeding to foreclose a mortgage on or to repossess personal property, or to rescind or terminate a contract for the purchase of personal property."[111] In such a case, the trial court is empowered to appoint three appraisers to determine the value of the personal property involved. Based on the appraised value, the court may order whatever sum, if any, it believes is representative of the servicemember's equity to be paid to the servicemember or the servicemember's dependent. This payment may be made a condition precedent to foreclosing the mortgage, terminating the contract, or permitting the vendor to resume possession of the chattel. This section has been effectively employed in the situation where the value of the pledged chattel is "rapidly diminishing."[112]

When applying 50 U.S.C. app. § 534, the trial court is faced with the task of striking a delicate balance of the equities between the servicemember, in whose favor a ruling previously has been made by way of a stay or proceedings, and the vendor, who has neither been paid nor has the benefit of the possession of the chattel. The dependents of the servicemember should not be subjected to undue hardship as a result of losing use of the chattel. Thus, their interest should be taken into consideration as well.

In fact, the sole restriction against the court's use of this section is embodied in the clause "if undue hardship to the servicemember's dependents will not result." "Undue hardship" is difficult to define. Therefore, the courts have considered it a factual determination that must be made on a case-by-case basis.[113]

[110] 50 U.S.C. app. § 534.

[111] *Id.* § 534(a).

[112] *See* S & C Motors v. Carden, 264 S.W.2d 627, 629 (1954).

[113] Commercial Sec. Co. v. Kavanaugh, 13 So.2d 533 (La. App., 1943).

IX. Storage Liens

Similar to other Title III protections is one involving foreclosure of storage liens:

50 U.S.C. app. § 537

(a) Liens.

(1) Limitation on foreclosure or enforcement. A person holding a lien on the property or effects of a servicemember may not, during any period of military service of the servicemember and for 90 days thereafter, foreclose or enforce any lien on such property or effects without a court order granted before foreclosure or enforcement.

(2) Lien defined. For the purposes of paragraph (1), the term "lien" includes a lien for storage, repair, or cleaning of the property or effects of a servicemember or a lien on such property or effects for any other reason.

(b) Stay of proceedings. In a proceeding to foreclose or enforce a lien subject to this section, the court may on its own motion, and shall if requested by a servicemember whose ability to comply with the obligation resulting in the proceeding is materially affected by military service—

(1) stay the proceeding for a period of time as justice and equity require; or

(2) adjust the obligation to preserve the interests of all parties. The provisions of this subsection do not affect the scope of section 303 [50 U.S.C. app. § 533].

(c) Penalties.

(1) Misdemeanor. A person who knowingly takes an action contrary to this section, or attempts to do so, shall be fined as provided in title 18, United States Code, or imprisoned for not more than one year, or both.

(2) Preservation of other remedies. The remedy and rights provided under this section are in addition to and do not preclude any remedy for wrongful conversion otherwise available under law to the person claiming relief under this section, including any consequential or punitive damages.[114]

Congress included this section to ensure judicial safeguards in all foreclosure proceedings and to avoid the possibility that summary foreclosures allowed by some states would be held without the SCRA protections. This section pertains to the foreclosure of liens for storage of household goods or other personal property of military personnel, whether the goods were stored prior to entry upon active duty or not. Such foreclosure is prohibited during the period of military service and for 90 days thereafter, unless the lienholder obtains an order from a court and a return is made and approved by the court.[115] Criminal penalties and civil remedies are provided, to punitive damages.[116]

[114] 50 U.S.C. app. § 537.

[115] *Id.* app. § 537(a)(1).

[116] *Id.* app. § 537(c). *See, e.g.*, United States v. Bomar, 8 F.3d 226 (5th Cir. 1993) (storage liens and criminal sanctions).

X. *Anticipatory Relief*

Like the Title III benefits and protections, the non-Title III section of the SCRA calling for "anticipatory relief" is potentially quite powerful. Unlike the Title III provisions and many of the SCRA's main provisions, it has been rarely invoked.

50 U.S.C. app. § 591

(a) Application for relief. A servicemember may, during military service or within 180 days of termination of or release from military service, apply to a court for relief—

(1) from any obligation or liability incurred by the servicemember before the servicemember's military service; or

(2) from a tax or assessment falling due before or during the servicemember's military service.

(b) Tax liability or assessment. In a case covered by subsection (a), the court may, if the ability of the servicemember to comply with the terms of such obligation or liability or pay such tax or assessment has been materially affected by reason of military service, after appropriate notice and hearing, grant the following relief:

- (1) Stay of enforcement of real estate contracts.
  - (A) In the case of an obligation payable in installments under a contract for the purchase of real estate, or secured by a mortgage or other instrument in the nature of a mortgage upon real estate, the court may grant a stay of the enforcement of the obligation—
    - (i) during the servicemember's period of military service; and
    - (ii) from the date of termination of or release from military service, or from the date of application if made after termination of or release from military service.
  - (B) Any stay under this paragraph shall be—
    - (i) for a period equal to the remaining life of the installment contract or other instrument, plus a period of time equal to the period of military service of the servicemember, or any part of such combined period; and
    - (ii) subject to payment of the balance of the principal and accumulated interest due and unpaid at the date of termination or release from the applicant's military service or from the date of application in equal installments during the combined period at the rate of interest on the unpaid balance prescribed in the contract or other instrument evidencing the obligation, and subject to other terms as may be equitable.
- (2) Stay of enforcement of other contracts.
  - (A) In the case of any other obligation, liability, tax, or assessment, the court may grant a stay of enforcement—
    - (i) during the servicemember's military service; and

(ii) from the date of termination of or release from military service, or from the date of application if made after termination or release from military service.

(B) Any stay under this paragraph shall be—

(i) for a period of time equal to the period of the servicemember's military service or any part of such period; and

(ii) subject to payment of the balance of principal and accumulated interest due and unpaid at the date of termination or release from military service, or the date of application, in equal periodic installments during this extended period at the rate of interest as may be prescribed for this obligation, liability, tax, or assessment, if paid when due, and subject to other terms as may be equitable.

(c) Affect of stay on fine or penalty. When a court grants a stay under this section, a fine or penalty shall not accrue on the obligation, liability, tax, or assessment for the period of compliance with the terms and conditions of the stay.[117]

The dearth of reported litigation in this area is probably due to the fact that servicemembers who are materially affected in their ability to meet their contractual obligations rarely have the opportunity to bring suit for declaratory relief. Be that as it may, this section provides a means by which a person in military service may orderly liquidate obligations and liabilities affected by that service. Unlike other provisions, it permits the servicemember to initiate the action instead of waiting for the creditor to commence proceedings.[118] Dependents do not have independent protection under this section, as they do for Title III protections.[119]

A court may suspend enforcement of all or any portion of any obligation or liability that arose prior to entry on active duty, or any tax or assessment falling due either before or during service. To obtain relief, the servicemember must apply to the court during his/her military service, or within six months thereafter, and satisfy the court that his/her ability to meet his/her obligations are materially affected by his/her service.

This section includes all contracts and mortgages plus any other obligation or liability incurred prior to entry on active duty or any tax or assessment regardless of when the tax or assessment falls due. The servicemember may apply for relief even if s/he is not in default on the obligation. The stay under this section may be for a longer period of time than under other sections of the Act.[120] For the purposes of relief, the

[117] 50 U.S.C. app. § 591.

[118] Kindy v. Koenke, 216 F.2d 907 (8th Cir. 1954).

[119] The Title III protections are discussed *supra* in this chapter. *See generally* 50 U.S.C. app. §§ 531-38.

[120] *See, e.g. id.* app. § 522 (general stay provision).

section is divided into two categories. The first involves obligations incurred "for the purchase of real estate[ ] or secured by a mortgage or other instrument in the nature of a mortgage upon real estate,"[121] and the second concerns "any other obligation, liability, tax, or assessment."[122]

To obtain relief under this section, the servicemember is required to apply to the court.[123] No court, as yet, has granted relief on its own motion under the provisions of this section. The question, however, of whether or not a servicemember is entitled to a stay where there is no default and no action pending was raised in *Application of Marks*.[124] In that case, the court decided that no action need be pending and the servicemember need not be in default. Additionally, the servicemember is not prohibited from applying for relief after action has been brought or a stay granted under other provisions of the act[125] such those involving installment contracts[126] and mortgage foreclosures.[127]

Once the court is satisfied that the servicemember's ability to meet his/her obligations is materially affected by his/her service, it has authority not only to stay the enforcement of the obligation, but also to set up an equitable plan or schedule for him/her to repay the debts he/she is unable to handle because of military service.

The stay provisions of this section provide that if the obligation involved is for the purchase of real estate or is secured by real estate, the court may grant a stay to allow the servicemember to suspend all payments while in service. The servicemember may then make up these back payments, plus interest, by spreading them out equally over the remaining life of the contract, plus a period of time equal to his/her time in service. For all other debts, the time allowable to make up the back payments cannot exceed a period of time equal to his/her time in service.

An example provides the best explanation of these provisions. Assume that when *A* enters the service, he owns a mortgaged house with 20 years remaining on the mortgage, and a boat with 5 years of installment payments remaining. While spending two years on active duty, he made reduced payments on both obligations by obtaining a stay under this section. When he is separated from the service, he has 18 more years on his mortgage and is $1400.00 in arrears. He also has three years of payments remaining on his boat and is $800.00 in arrears on this debt. The court may allow the $1400.00 to be spread out for a period of 20 years and the $800.00 for a period of two years. The maximum permissible period for the stay on the mortgage is calculated by

[121] *Id.* app. § 591(b)(1)(A).
[122] *Id.* app. § 591(b)(2)(A).
[123] *Id.* app. § 591(a).
[124] 46 N.Y.S.2d 755 (N.Y. Sup. Ct. 1944). *See also* Peterson v. Shaffer, 352 P.2d 281 (1960) (military service did not materially affect servicemember).
[125] New York Life Ins. Co. v. Litke, 41 N.Y.S.2d 526, *modified on other grounds*, 45 N.Y.S.2d 576 (N.Y. Sup. Ct. 1943).
[126] 50 U.S.C. app. § 532.
[127] *Id.* app. § 533.

adding the 18 years remaining on the mortgage at the time of separation to the two years *A* spent in the service. As to the installment contract on the boat, *A* could be permitted a maximum of 2 years to make up the arrears since the court is allowed to grant a stay equal to his term of service.

In addition, the discharged servicemember will be required to resume his regular payments at the same time he is paying the arrears. The stay described in the example is the maximum allowable stay. The court could order less time for repayment, in accordance with its equitable powers.[128]

[128] *See, e.g.*, Application of Pickard, 60 N.Y.S.2d 506 (1946).

Chapter 5

Taxation and Voting Rights

I. *Introduction*

This chapter considers two related sets of protections. The first involves the SCRA provisions related to taxation, to include taxes on income, personal property, and sales. The second involves a philosophically related area pertaining to voting rights of military personnel.

II. Residence for Tax Purposes

Military service typically involves performance of duty and stationing away from one's original home. In the following provision, Congress means to preclude the possibility that servicemembers will have their income and personal property taxed by their home state and by the state where they are stationed.

50 U.S.C. app. § 571

(a) Residence or domicile. A servicemember shall neither lose nor acquire a residence or domicile for purposes of taxation with respect to the person, personal property, or income of the servicemember by reason of being absent or present in any tax jurisdiction of the United States solely in compliance with military orders.

(b) Military service compensation. Compensation of a servicemember for military service shall not be deemed to be income for services performed or from sources within a tax jurisdiction of the United States if the servicemember is not a resident or domiciliary of the jurisdiction in which the servicemember is serving in compliance with military orders.

(c) Personal property.

  (1) Relief from personal property taxes. The personal property of a servicemember shall not be deemed to be located or present in, or to have a situs for taxation in, the tax jurisdiction in which the servicemember is serving in compliance with military orders.

  (2) Exception for property within member's domicile or residence. This subsection applies to personal property or its use within any tax jurisdiction other than the servicemember's domicile or residence.

(3) Exception for property used in trade or business. This section does not prevent taxation by a tax jurisdiction with respect to personal property used in or arising from a trade or business, if it has jurisdiction.
(4) Relationship to law of state of domicile. Eligibility for relief from personal property taxes under this subsection is not contingent on whether or not such taxes are paid to the State of domicile.

(d) Increase of tax liability. A tax jurisdiction may not use the military compensation of a nonresident servicemember to increase the tax liability imposed on other income earned by the nonresident servicemember or spouse subject to tax by the jurisdiction.
(e) Federal Indian reservations. An Indian servicemember whose legal residence or domicile is a Federal Indian reservation shall be taxed by the laws applicable to Federal Indian reservations and not the State where the reservation is located.
(f) Definitions. For purposes of this section:
(1) Personal property. The term "personal property" means intangible and tangible property (including motor vehicles).
(2) Taxation. The term "taxation" includes licenses, fees, or excises imposed with respect to motor vehicles and their use, if the license, fee, or excise is paid by the servicemember in the servicemember's State of domicile or residence.
(3) Tax jurisdiction. The term "tax jurisdiction" means a State or a political subdivision of a State.[1]

A. General

Section 571 provides that a servicemember neither acquires nor loses residence or domicile solely by residing in a given state pursuant to military orders. For taxation purposes, it creates two important fictions. First, a servicemember's income is deemed earned in the home state, even the though servicemember is working in another state. Second, a servicemember's personal property is deemed located in the home state rather then in the host state where the servicemember is actually stationed. These "statutory fictions" are critical when applying generally accepted taxation rules to military personnel.[2] By establishing these fictions, section 571, in effect, prevents multiple taxation of the servicemember's military income and personal property by various taxing jurisdictions.[3]

[1] 50 U.S.C.S. app. § 571 (LEXIS 2006).

[2] Generally, a state can tax all income, from whatever source derived, of domiciliaries and statutory residents. With respect to nonresidents, states generally may tax all income earned within the state. *See* Jerome R. Hellerstein & Walter Hellerstein, State And Local Taxation 856-860 (6th ed 1997) (explaining constitutional allowances of state income taxation of individuals) and 872-876 (discussing residence and domicile with respect to taxing power). *See also* New York *ex rel.* Cohn v. Graves, 300 U.S. 308 (1937).

[3] The forerunner to section 571 was section 574 of the old SSCRA, which was substantially similar to section 571. The Supreme Court upheld the constitutionality of section 574 of the SSCRA. *See* Dameron v. Brodhead, 345 U.S. 322 (1953).

Attorneys should note that servicemembers and their family members frequently misunderstand the scope of taxation protections under the section. Servicemembers frequently wrongly believe that their military income is exempt from all taxation, to include taxation by their state of domicile. They may also wrongly believe that the SCRA exempts their nonmilitary income from taxation. In this regard it is critical for legal assistance practitioners to be diligent in emphasizing what the SCRA does and does not protect. For example, if a servicemember acquires a second, part-time job, the income from that pursuit is fully taxable where earned.[4] Similarly, personal property used in a trade or business is outside the SCRA's reach.[5]

B. Income Tax

Unless it is also the servicemember's home state, the host state may not tax the compensation the servicemember receives "for military service"[6] because this compensation "shall not be deemed to be income for services performed"[7] in the host state. This is the statutory exception to the general rule that states may tax all income earned within the state.

With regard to taxation of Native American servicemembers whose domicile is a Federal Indian reservation, section 571 clarifies an issue not specifically addressed under the old SSCRA. Pursuant to federal law, the income of a resident of a federal reservation is generally not taxable by the state. Previously, under the SSCRA, some states argued that income earned by Native Americans while in the military was income earned off the reservation, and thus taxable by the home state.[8] Although the states were generally unsuccessful with the argument, Congress headed off future disputes by stating in section 571 that Native American servicemembers shall be taxed by the laws applicable to the reservation and not the state where the reservation is located.[9]

C. Spouse's Income and Personal Property

A spouse's income is not protected under section 571, nor is the spouse's personal property. Any of the spouse's income, earned in the state where the servicemember is

[4] 50 U.S.C.S. app. § 571(b)(limits the protection to "[c]ompensation . . . for military service"). An interesting issue arises when a servicemember earns nonmilitary income in a state other than the host state, such as when the servicemember has an off-duty job in a state adjoining his/her military installation. In that situation the host state may not tax the income because the servicemember is a nonresident under section 571 with respect to the host state. The host state may only tax residents on income earned within its boundaries. *See* New York *ex rel.* Whitney v. Graves, 299 U.S. 366 (1937).

[5] 50 U.S.C.S. app. § 571(c)(3).

[6] *Id.* app. §571(b).

[7] *Id.*

[8] *See* Fatt v. Utah, 884 P.2d 1233 (Ut. 1994).

[9] 50 U.S.C.S. app. § 571(e) (LEXIS 2006).

stationed, is fully taxable.[10] However, with the passage of the SCRA a significant change came about regarding the practice used by some states to calculate the spouse's state income tax *rate*. In the past, some states included the servicemember's non-taxable military income when determining the rate at which the spouse's income was to be taxed.[11] Although these states did not directly tax the servicemember's nonmilitary income, they added the military income to the spouse's income for purposes of determining the spouse's income tax bracket. In many instances, this practice placed the spouse's taxable income in a higher tax bracket, resulting in the application of a higher tax rate to much of the spouse's taxable income. The new SCRA specifically prohibits this practice.[12]

In situations where the servicemember, his/her dependent, or both, are properly subject to taxation by two or more states, the servicemember and dependents may be eligible for tax credits. Generally, this is a credit against the tax of the home state in the amount of the tax paid to the state where the income was earned. There may be amount limitations or other formulas to determine the amount of the credit. Another form of tax credit occurs when the state in which the income is earned gives the non-resident taxpayer credit for tax on the income paid in the home state. In either case, state statutes are generally worded to prevent the tax credit from being taken twice. Other forms of relief may consist of an exclusion or deduction of the income from the gross income reported to the home state when tax was paid to the state where it was earned, or merely an itemized deduction of the tax paid to the other state.

D. Tangible Nonbusiness Personal Property

Section 571(c)(1) states that for purposes of taxation, nonbusiness personal property "shall not be deemed to be located or present in, or to have a situs for taxation" in the host state. This section does not, however, extend protection to the property owned by the servicemember's dependents. Examples of, and exceptions to, this general rule follow:

[10] Nonmilitary spouses and other military dependents potentially may be taxed by (1) the home state, (2) the host state, and (3) the state where the income is earned, such as when the duty station is near a state boundary and the income is earned in the adjoining state. If the state where the income is earned is other than the host state, the only theory upon which the host state could tax is that the nonmilitary spouse or dependent acquired a statutory residence in the host state. Attorneys should examine the law of the host state to determine if the nonmilitary spouse or dependent acquires a residence for tax purposes.

[11] United States v. Kansas, 580 F. Supp. 512 (D. Kan. 1984), *aff'd*, 810 F.2d 935 (10th Cir. 1987). Prior to its elimination by the 2003 SCRA, the so-called "Kansas Rule" was followed by the states of California, Kansas, Missouri, Nebraska, Utah, and Vermont. *See* Robert L. Minor, *"Inclusion of Nonresident Military Income In State Apportionment of Income Formulas: Violation of the Soldiers' and Sailors' Civil Relief Act?,"* 102 MIL. L. REV. 97 (1983).

[12] 50 U.S.C. app. § 571(d).

1. Sales and use taxes

In *Sullivan v. United States*,[13] the Supreme Court held that section 574 of the old SSCRA[14] (the section substantially similar to section 571 of the SCRA), does not exempt servicemembers from sales and use taxes imposed by states other than the home state. The court determined that sales and use taxes are not imposed on the property itself. Rather, a sales tax is an excise imposed upon the sale transaction, and a use tax is "in the nature of an excise upon the privilege of using, storing or consuming property."[15] Further, the Court held that Congress intended to limit protection of servicemembers' personal property, stating that only "annually recurring taxes on property—[including] the familiar *ad valorem* personal property tax,"[16] are prohibited.[17] Finally, the Court noted that Congressional action in the Buck Act of 1940[18] dealt specifically with sales and use taxes.[19] The Act authorized state authorities to collect such taxes on land subject to federal jurisdiction,[20] except for sale or use of property sold by the United States or its instrumentalities through a commissary, a ship store, or the like.[21]

While the *Sullivan* case is clear that a tax on the sales transaction, whether it is called a sales or use tax, may be imposed by the state, the question remains whether a servicemember's personal property is subject to such a tax each time he/she moves the property to a new state. Servicemembers should retain evidence of sales taxes paid on the purchase of major items, such as automobiles, to avoid further taxation upon relocation. Ordinarily a credit in the amount of the sales tax paid will be given by the authority imposing the use tax. Because this is strictly a state function, there is no federal assurance that states will grant a credit or exemption for sales taxes paid.[22]

[13] Sullivan v. United States, 395 U.S. 169 (1969).

[14] 50 U.S.C. app. § 574 (2000).

[15] *Sullivan*, 395 U.S. at 177 (quoting Connecticut Light & Power Co. v. Walsh, 57 A.2d 128, 134 (1948).

[16] *Sullivan* , 395 U.S. at 176.

[17] *See infra* para. 5-2d(2) for further discussion of *ad valorem* taxes.

[18] 4 U.S.C.S. §§ 105-110 (LEXIS 2006).

[19] Sullivan, 395 U.S. at 178.

[20] 4 U.S.C.S. § 105(a).

[21] *Id.* § 107.

[22] Connecticut, for example, allows nonresident military members and their spouses to purchase motor vehicles with a reduced sales/use tax. *See* State of Connecticut Policy Statement, "Sales of Motor Vehicles to Nonresident Military Personnel and Joint Sales of Motor Vehicles to Nonresident Military Personnel and Their Spouses," PS 2001(4), 2001 Conn. Tax LEXIS 16 (April 20, 2001). *See also*, Nebraska Attorney General Opinion No. 99043, "Taxation of Motor Vehicles of Active Duty Military Personnel Stationed in Nebraska," 1999 STT 198-11 (September 27, 1999) (detailing the rules for taxation of vehicles owned by active duty servicemembers in Nebraska, and opining that a military member who purchases a **motor vehicle** in Nebraska or elsewhere is not required to pay Nebraska **sales** or use tax if the vehicle is registered in the member's home state).

2. Ad valorem tax

The term "ad valorem tax" is defined as "a tax imposed proportionally on the value of something . . ."[23] or a "tax or duty upon the value of the article or thing subject to taxation."[24] A prime example of an *ad valorem* tax is a state's annual tax on the value of a motor vehicle operating on the public highways of that state.[25] The Supreme Court in *Sullivan* was absolute in holding that *ad valorem* personal property taxes, whether on motor vehicles or other personal property, by the host state were prohibited by the SSCRA.[26] The right to impose this tax is reserved to the home state.[27] Nothing in the new SCRA changes this analysis.

(a) **Constructive placement.** Because the SCRA allows the use of the fiction that personal property is not in the place where it is physically located for the purpose of assessing an *ad valorem* tax, the home state could arguably apply a reverse fiction in finding its legal presence for tax purposes in a place where it is not. The application of this fiction may, however, have practical drawbacks, especially where the tax assessor must see the property in order to set a tax.

(b) **Jointly Held Personal Property/Community Property.** Frequently, nonmilitary spouses are included on the title of taxable personal property items (e.g. a boat, trailer, or motor vehicle) as joint owners or having community property ownership. In this situation, the protection from host state taxation of personal property under section 571 is probably defeated.[28] The Act mentions only the "servicemember" when declaring that domicile is neither lost nor acquired solely based on military assignment. As a result, most states take the position that jointly owned personal property may be taxed by the state of domicile as well as the host state. [29]

(c) **Mobile Homes.** Under the SSCRA, if the host state treated a mobile home as tangible nonbusiness personal property, the mobile home had the same protection as a motor vehicle or any other such property with regard to ad valorem taxes imposed by the host state.[30] Section 571 of the SCRA is substan-

[23] BLACK'S LAW DICTIONARY 1469 (7th ed. 1999).

[24] Arthur v. Johnson, 185 S.C. 324, 327, 194 S.E. 151, 154 (1937).

[25] *See infra* para. 5-3 for additional coverage of taxation of motor vehicles under the SCRA.

[26] Sullivan v. United States, 395 U.S. 169, 176 (1969).

[27] 50 U.S.C. app. § 571(c)(2) (stating that the personal property tax protections of the SCRA apply to tax jurisdictions other than the servicemember's domicile).

[28] Generally, courts have held that the spouse/dependents of a servicemember are not entitled to the benefits of the SSCRA (or SCRA). *See* Lester v. United States, 487 F. Supp. 1033, 1039 (N.D. Tex. 1980); Card v. Am. Brands Corp., 401 F. Supp. 1186, 1188 (S.D. N.Y. 1975); Buttler v. City of Los Angeles, 200 Cal. Rptr. 372 ((Cal. App. 2d Dist. 1984).

[29] *See generally*, Lieutenant Colonel Paul Conrad, *Nonmilitary Spouse's Joint Ownership of Personal Property Voids Soldiers' Civil Relief Act Personal Property Tax Protection*, ARMY LAW., August 1997, at 24.

[30] Snapp v. Neal, 382 U.S. 397 (1966); United States v. Illinois, 525 F.2d 374 (7th Cir. 1975) (mobile home is personal property under Illinois law; county could not impose personal property tax on mobile homes owned by nonresident servicemembers).

tially similar to the SSCRA provision and preserves the same protections.[31] Legal assistance practitioners should be aware, however, that if the law of the host state classifies the mobile home as a motor vehicle, registration with its accompanying license, fee, or excise may be imposed if the servicemember has not complied with the registration requirements of the home state.[32]

E. Intangible Nonbusiness Personal Property

The definition of personal property under section 571(f)(1) includes "intangible and tangible property." Definitions of intangible personal property traditionally include stocks, bonds, and bank deposits.[33] Section 571(c)(1) is clear that the personal property of a servicemember shall not have a situs for taxation in the host state, meaning the intangible personal property cannot be taxed by the host state.[34] A related issue is taxation of the *income* derived from this property. Traditionally, income derived from personal property is taxed by the owner's legal domicile.[35] As a result, with regard to taxation of intangible personal property itself (an *ad valorem* tax), as well as the income derived thereof, the servicemember is protected under section 571 from taxation by the host state.

F. Property Used in a Trade or Business

Section 571(c)(3) does not prevent taxation of property used by a servicemember or dependent in a trade or business. Therefore, the value and income of business property used by a servicemember in the host state is fully taxable in accordance with host state law.

G. Real Property

The protections of section 571 against host state taxation apply only to the servicemember's military income and personal property. Section 571 does not apply to real property.[36] The traditional rule is that real property is taxed only by the state in

[31] 50 U.S.C. app. § 571(c)(1).

[32] For further discussion of taxation of motor vehicles, see *infra* para. 5-3a.

[33] *See* Black's Law Dictionary 1233 (7th ed. 1999) (defining intangible property as "Property that lacks a physical existence. Examples include bank accounts, stock options, and business goodwill.")

[34] Traditionally, intangibles have as their situs the domicile of the owner. *See* Wheeling Steel Corp. v. Fox, 298 U.S. 193, 209 (1936).

[35] Suttles v. Illinois Glass Co., 206 Ga. 849, 59 S.E.2d 394 (1950).

[36] In interpreting the forerunner of section 571 under the old SSCRA (50 U.S.C. App. § 574), the Fourth Circuit held that the SSCRA did not apply to the taxation of real property since it "only reaches state taxation of income and personal property. . . . Congress did not include real property taxes within the statutory prohibition; real property can have but a single situs for tax purposes." *See* United States v. Onslow Co. Bd.. of Education, 728 F.2d 628, 636 (4th Cir. 1984). Further, the Supreme Court has held that "Congress intended the Act to cover only annually recurring taxes on property—the familiar ad valorem personal property tax." *See* Sullivan v. United States, 395 U.S. 169, 176-77 (1969).

which it is situated. Therefore, it is not affected by the servicemember's status (whether a domiciliary or merely a temporary resident based on military orders).

III. *Motor Vehicle Taxation and Driver's Licenses*

A. Motor Vehicle Taxation

Section 571(f)(2) provides that the term "taxation" includes "licenses, fees, or excises imposed with respect to motor vehicles and their use" but only if the servicemember paid the license, fee, or excise required by the servicemember's home state. In effect, as long as the servicemember has registered and licensed his vehicle in the home state, and paid applicable fees, he is free from the licensing, registration and associated fee requirements of the host state. It is important to note that in order to gain the protections of section 571, the servicemember must have actually licensed and registered the vehicle in the home state, even though the home state may exempt the servicemember from registration and licensing requirements when the vehicle will not be driven in the home state.

In *California v. Buzard*,[37] the Supreme Court, in analyzing a similar provision of the old SSCRA, held that even though a home state exempted a resident from licensing and fee requirements when the vehicle was not driven in the home state, the servicemember would have to register and license the vehicle in his home state in order to qualify for the exemption under the SSCRA. If a servicemember does not pay to license and register his car in the home state, the host state may require him to pay in order to register his vehicle in the host state. The servicemember does not, however, have to pay the entire amount assessed if a portion of the license, fee or excise exceeds the amount necessary to register and license the vehicle. Fees in excess of the cost of issuance and administration are barred by section 571. In *Buzard*, the court held that the excessive amount is an *ad valorem* tax that may not be imposed by the host state upon a servicemember's personal property. This specifically included motor vehicles.[38]

Thus, for purposes of section 571, taxation in relation to motor vehicles must be analyzed under two categories. First, as a piece of tangible non-business property, the motor vehicle is exempt from *ad valorem* taxes under section 571(c)(1) regardless of the desire of the host state to tax it. Second, as a machine that moves on the streets and highways of the host state, it is subject to the police power of the host state. A host state may exercise its police power to require a servicemember to register a vehicle in its jurisdiction if, and only if, the servicemember has not registered the vehicle in the home state.

Because section 571 applies to "any tax jurisdiction of the United States,"[39] a similar analysis applies to attempts by local municipalities and political subdivi-

[37] California v. Buzard, 382 U.S. 386 (1966).

[38] *Id.* at 392. The host state attempted to impose an $8.00 standard fee which was held reasonable and a $100.00 fee based upon the value of the vehicle. The latter fee was determined to be an *ad valorem* tax.

[39] 50 U.S.C. app. § 571(a) (LEXIS 2006).

sions to tax the servicemember's vehicle. So long as the requirements of the home state are met, a political subdivision has no greater right than the host state to impose its own requirements. In addition, the nonresident servicemember is exempt from paying revenue-raising taxes regardless of whether he paid similar taxes in the state of domicile.[40]

B. Driver's Licenses

The SCRA does not preclude states from requiring persons who live within their borders to acquire a driver's license. Some states, however, allow servicemembers to retain their license if issued from their home state.[41] Also, some states exempt the servicemember's spouse and dependents from the state's licensing requirements.[42]

IV. Deferral of Collection of Income Taxes

Servicemembers receive a number of tax breaks independent of the SCRA, especially those deployed to a combat zone.[43] Section 570 of the SCRA provides an additional, oft overlooked, protection:

50 U.S.C. app. § 570

(a) Deferral of tax. Upon notice to the Internal Revenue Service or the tax authority of a State or a political subdivision of a State, the collection of income tax on the income of a servicemember falling due before or during

[40] 50 U.S.C. app. § 571(c)(4). *See also* United States v. City of Highwood, 712 F. Supp. 138 (N.D. Ill. 1989) (city could not require nonresident Fort Sheridan soldiers to pay revenue raising fee on vehicles operated within the city. The court also held that the city erroneously attributed automobile registration to a change of domicile).

[41] *See generally* FLA. STAT.§ 322.03 (Matthew Bender & Co., Inc., LEXISNEXIS through 2005 Special Session B); N.C. GEN. STAT. § 20-8 (Matthew Bender & Co., Inc., LEXISNEXIS through 2005 legislation); IDAHO CODE § 49-302 (Matthew Bender & Co., Inc., LEXISNEXIS through 2005 legislation); 625 ILL. COMP. STAT. 5/6-102 (.(Matthew Bender & Co., Inc., LEXISNEXIS through 2005 legislation); MONT.CODE ANN. § 61-5-104 (LEXISNEXIS through 2005 special session).

[42] *See* N.C. GEN. STAT. § 20-8 (Matthew Bender & Co., Inc., LEXISNEXIS through 2005 legislation) (specifically exempts nonresident military spouses from host state license requirements, regardless of their employment status, who are temporarily residing in North Carolina due to the active duty military orders of a spouse); LA. REV. STAT. ANN § 32:404 (Matthew Bender & Co., Inc., LEXISNEXIS through 2005 regular legislative session) (exempts resident military dependents from host state license requirements if in possession of a valid home state license and a military dependent identification card).

[43] A detailed discussion of those protections is beyond the scope of this publication. However, some of the more common tax-related benefits enjoyed by many deployed servicemembers include the extension of time to file tax returns, exclusion of income received in a combat zone from gross income, and numerous tax benefits related to servicemembers dying in a combat zone. *See* Major Richard W. Rousseau, *Update: Tax Benefits for Military Personnel in a Combat Zone or Qualified Hazardous Duty Areas*, ARMY LAW., Dec. 1999, at 1.

military service shall be deferred for a period not more than 180 days after termination of or release from military service, if a servicemember's ability to pay such income tax is materially affected by military service.

(b) Accrual of interest or penalty. No interest or penalty shall accrue for the period of deferment by reason of nonpayment on any amount of tax deferred under this section.

(c) Statute of limitations. The running of a statute of limitations against the collection of tax deferred under this section, by seizure or otherwise, shall be suspended for the period of military service of the servicemember and for an additional period of 270 days thereafter.

(d) Application limitation. This section shall not apply to the tax imposed on employees by section 3101 of the Internal Revenue Code of 1986 [26 USCS § 3101].[44]

A. General

This section defers collection of any income tax, federal or state, on military or non-military income, falling due either before or during military service. Unlike certain other tax benefits, this section requires that the servicemember show material effect. It is not automatic, but may have utility for servicemembers who are deployed to non-combat zones and at such times when it may be difficult for them to file tax returns.

B. State Income Tax

Servicemembers seeking relief from state income taxes should apply to the local tax authority or the state attorney general and cite section 570.

C. Filing Tax Returns

Section 570 grants relief from tax collection but not from *filing* returns. An extension or postponement of the time for filing may, however, be authorized under other authority. For example, personnel on duty overseas are authorized an automatic extension of two months (or longer if granted permission) for filing federal income tax returns.[45] Personnel on duty in a combat zone are authorized to postpone filing their federal income tax returns for the duration of combat service plus 180 days.[46] Several states provide similar relief for military personnel in filing state income tax returns.

V. *Non-Income Personal and Real Property Taxes*

A final tax provision, of some consequence, concerns taxes owed on personal and real property.

[44] 50 U.S.C. app. § 570.
[45] Treas. Reg. § 1.6081-5(a)(6).
[46] I.R.C. § 7508(a)(1) (2005).

50 U.S.C. app. § 561

(a) Application. This section applies in any case in which a tax or assessment, whether general or special (other than a tax on personal income), falls due and remains unpaid before or during a period of military service with respect to a servicemember's—
  (1) personal property (including motor vehicles); or
  (2) real property occupied for dwelling, professional, business, or agricultural purposes by a servicemember or the servicemember's dependents or employees—
    (A) before the servicemember's entry into military service; and
    (B) during the time the tax or assessment remains unpaid.

(b) Sale of property.
  (1) Limitation on sale of property to enforce tax assessment. Property described in subsection (a) may not be sold to enforce the collection of such tax or assessment except by court order and upon the determination by the court that military service does not materially affect the servicemember's ability to pay the unpaid tax or assessment.
  (2) Stay of court proceedings. A court may stay a proceeding to enforce the collection of such tax or assessment, or sale of such property, during a period of military service of the servicemember and for a period not more than 180 days after the termination of, or release of the servicemember from, military service.

(c) Redemption. When property described in subsection (a) is sold or forfeited to enforce the collection of a tax or assessment, a servicemember shall have the right to redeem or commence an action to redeem the servicemember's property during the period of military service or within 180 days after termination of or release from military service. This subsection may not be construed to shorten any period provided by the law of a State (including any political subdivision of a State) for redemption.

(d) Interest on tax or assessment. Whenever a servicemember does not pay a tax or assessment on property described in subsection (a) when due, the amount of the tax or assessment due and unpaid shall bear interest until paid at the rate of 6 percent per year. An additional penalty or interest shall not be incurred by reason of nonpayment. A lien for such unpaid tax or assessment may include interest under this subsection.

(e) Joint ownership application. This section applies to all forms of property described in subsection (a) owned individually by a servicemember or jointly by a servicemember and a dependent or dependents.[47]

A. General

Section 561 involves the sale of property resulting from tax deficiencies as well as subsequent redemption rights. Taxes include any tax or assessment, whether special or

[47] 50 U.S.C. app. § 561.

general, due before or during the period of military service. It does not include income taxes. The Act specifically protects personal property, to include motor vehicles.

The Act also protects real property, as long as the real property was occupied for dwelling, professional, business, or agricultural purposes by a servicemember or the servicemember's dependents or employees. The occupation must have been *before* the servicemember's entry into military service; and *during* the time the tax or assessment remains unpaid. The term "occupied" was strictly construed by one court under the old SSCRA. Where the servicemember never resided on the land, farmed it, raised livestock on it, or leased it to another for agricultural purposes, but merely inspected it periodically for trespassers, the court held that the servicemember was not in "occupation of the land for agricultural purposes"[48] and, therefore, not protected under the SSCRA against the sale for nonpayment of taxes.

B. Protection Provided

Property may not be sold to enforce a tax assessment against the servicemember without a court order, and then only when the court determines that the military service does not materially affect the servicemembers's ability to pay. In interpreting a section under the old SSCRA that was substantially similar to section 561 of the SCRA, the Florida Supreme Court held that a deed issued in violation of the SSCRA section was voidable.[49] In another case involving the old SSCRA, the Utah Supreme Court held that a grantee under such a void tax deed had no cause of action against a servicemember for improvements the grantee placed on the land in reliance on the deed. The grantee had been notified that a person protected by the SSCRA owned the property.[50]

C. Right of Redemption

In cases where the property may be lawfully sold to satisfy taxes or assessments, section 561(c) gives the servicemember time in which to redeem the property. Redemption action must begin within 180 days after termination of or release from military service, or a later date if a greater redemption period is authorized by the laws of the state or territory. The ability to pay need not be materially affected by military service for section 561(c) to apply.

If relief under section 561 is inappropriate, either because more than 180 days have passed since termination of military service, or because the property is not one of the limited types listed in section 561(a), section 526 (Statute of Limitations) should be reviewed for possible relief. Section 526 suspends the time for computing the limitation of actions during the period of service. This includes the period "for the redemption of real property sold or forfeited to enforce an obligation, tax, or assess-

---

[48] Day v. Jones, 187 P.2d 181, 183 (1947).

[49] Moorman v. Thomas, 199 So.2d 719 (Fla. 1967).

[50] *See* Day v. Jones, 187 P.2d 181 (1947).

ment." Even if the property is not protected under section 561, the tolling provision of section 526 may still provide the servicemember an avenue of relief. In *Le Maistre v. Leffers*,[51] the Supreme Court held that the SSCRA's tolling provision is not restricted by section 525 (the SSCRA's equivalent provision to the current SCRA section 561); rather, they supplement each other.

VI. Voting Rights

In a provision similar to the one involving residency for income tax purposes, the SCRA protects a servicemember's right to vote in elections in his or her home state:

50 U.S.C. app. § 595

For the purposes of voting for any Federal office (as defined in section 301 of the Federal Election Campaign Act of 1971 [2 U.S.C. § 431] or a State or local office, a person who is absent from a State in compliance with military or naval orders shall not, solely by reason of that absence—

(1) be deemed to have lost a residence or domicile in that State, without regard to whether or not the person intends to return to that State;
(2) be deemed to have acquired a residence or domicile in any other State; or
(3) be deemed to have become a resident in or a resident of any other State.[52]

Similar to the taxation provisions under section 571, section 595 ensures that, *for voting purposes*, a servicemember neither acquires nor loses residence or domicile solely by residing in a given state pursuant to military orders. Unless the servicemember takes affirmative steps to register to vote in the host state, the servicemember's home state registration remains valid. Obviously, servicemembers should be cautioned about changing their voter registration to the host state, as this action could have ramifications beyond voting issues, especially with regard to residency for state income tax purposes. Although voter registration does not normally, by itself, establish residency for tax purposes, it is considered by most states to be an important factor in determining an individual's residency.[53]

[51] Le Maistre v. Leffers, 333 U.S. 1 (1948). *See also* Hedrick v. Bigby, 228 Ark. 40, 305 S.W.2d 674 (1957).

[52] 50 U.S.C. app. § 595.

[53] Captain [Albert] Veldhuyzen & Commander Samuel F. Wright, *Domicile of Military Personnel for Voting and Taxation*, Army Law., Sept. 1992, at 15.

Chapter 6

Financial Protections

I. *Introduction*

As previously mentioned, the SCRA can be thought of as providing procedural and substantive benefits. This chapter will discuss the remaining substantive benefits.

II. *Six Percent Interest Cap*

A. The Statute

The SCRA limits the interest on pre-service obligations through the following provision:

50 U.S.C. app. § 527

(a) Interest rate limitation.

(1) Limitation to 6 percent. An obligation or liability bearing interest at a rate in excess of 6 percent per year that is incurred by a servicemember, or the servicemember and the servicemember's spouse jointly, before the servicemember enters military service shall not bear interest at a rate in excess of 6 percent per year during the period of military service.

(2) Forgiveness of interest in excess of 6 percent. Interest at a rate in excess of 6 percent per year that would otherwise be incurred but for the prohibition in paragraph (1) is forgiven.

(3) Prevention of acceleration of principal. The amount of any periodic payment due from a servicemember under the terms of the instrument that created an obligation or liability covered by this section shall be reduced by the amount of the interest forgiven under paragraph (2) that is allocable to the period for which such payment is made.

(b) Implementation of limitation.

(1) Written notice to creditor. In order for an obligation or liability of a servicemember to be subject to the interest rate limitation in subsection (a), the servicemember shall provide to the creditor written notice and a copy of the military orders calling the servicemember to military service and any orders further extending military service, not later than 180 days after the date of the servicemember's termination or release from military service.

(2) Limitation effective as of date of order to active duty. Upon receipt of written notice and a copy of orders calling a servicemember to military service, the creditor shall treat the debt in accordance with subsection (a), effective as of the date on which the servicemember is called to military service.

(c) Creditor protection. A court may grant a creditor relief from the limitations of this section if, in the opinion of the court, the ability of the servicemember to pay interest upon the obligation or liability at a rate in excess of 6 percent per year is not materially affected by reason of the servicemember's military service.

(d) Interest. As used in this section, the term "interest" includes service charges, renewal charges, fees, or any other charges (except bona fide insurance) with respect to an obligation or liability.[1]

B. Six Percent Interest Benefit Basics

Just as the statute says, a servicemember can reduce interest on debts that existed prior to entry on active duty.[2] Even secured debts under a confirmed bankruptcy plan are subject to the benefit.[3] The benefit extends to cover debts jointly held with the servicemember's spouse. The point is to have the servicemember's payment reduced else there is little benefit. Although the servicemember must notify the creditor, the burden is on the creditor to show that the servicemember's military service does not materially impact her ability to pay the obligation.[4] "Interest" is broadly defined to preclude creditors from trying to collect the amount under another name. The interest is "forgiven," it is not deferred.

Under the prior provision, creditors often tried to hide the interest or to otherwise avoid the loss.[5] The current provision is straightforward. In comparison to the former provision,[6] the SCRA is abundantly clear. Nonetheless, it is important to be mindful of Congress' intent:

> To resolve lingering questions about congressional intent, section 207 [50 U.S.C. app. § 527] (dealing with the maximum rate of interest on debts incurred before military service) would clearly provide that interest above the 6 percent rate is to be forgiven, and that the amount of the monthly payment is to be reduced. Not to forgive interest above the 6 percent maximum rate would place the servicemember in precisely the same financial dilemma Congress

[1] 50 U.S.C.S. app. § 527 (LEXIS 2006).

[2] *Id.* app. § 511(2). For a discussion of the terminology of military service and active duty, *see supra* para. 2-2.

[3] *See, e.g.*, Baxter v. Watson (*In re* Watson), 292 B.R. 441, 444 (S.D.Ga. 2003).

[4] *Id.* at 445.

[5] *See, e.g.*, Major James Pottorff, *A Look at the Credit Industry's Approach to the Six Percent Limitation on Interest Rates*, ARMY LAW., Nov. 1990, at 49.

[6] *See* 50 U.S.C. app. § 526 (2000).

sought to ameliorate with the 1942 amendments. *See* H. Rept. 2198, 4 (1942). In addition, section 207 would clarify that joint debts between a servicemember and his or her spouse are entitled to the 6 percent interest relief protection.

The original section provided no guidance on how the servicemember should initiate an interest rate reduction. The Committee believes the burden should be on the servicemember to inform the creditor of the order for military service within a specific time. Section 207 would codify the practices established during the Persian Gulf War. The servicemember would be required to submit to the creditor written notice and a copy of military orders. These orders indicate the period of time for which the servicemember is called to duty. If there is an extension of the military duty obligation, the servicemember receives amended orders and would be required to provide the amended orders to the creditor in order to extend further the 6 percent protection. The Committee notes that, while the section would allow for notice to the creditor of up to 180 days after the servicemember's termination or release from military service, it would obviously be of advantage to servicemembers to provide notice to creditors more quickly so that their monthly payments are reduced during the period of military service when their income may be reduced.[7]

C. Six Percent Practical Considerations

Despite the fact that the burden of proof is on the creditor to show that the servicemember's military service does not affect the ability to pay at the higher rate of interest, it may be in the servicemember's best interest to explain how the military service has caused a negative impact.[8] Normally, the key aspect of the inquiry will be into the servicemember's finances. It will not stop, however, with a review of the servicemember's income. There are times when a person will experience an increase in income because of a mobilization, but the financial situation will worsen. Members activated from the reserve components may find they have two households to maintain and that child care and other expenses have likewise increased.

During a reserve component activation, reserve servicemembers regularly invoke the protection. It should be noted, however, that the benefit also extends to new active component officers and enlisted personnel. Active component servicemembers seldom invoke the provision because the obligation must predate the active service. Additionally, any material effect is apt to be positive. The financial well being of officers fresh from college and enlisted servicemembers from high school is often enhanced. The opposite is often true for many reserve personnel who leave well-paying civilian jobs for less lucrative military assignments.

The benefit is only for those debts which existed prior to the servicemember's entry on active duty. Debts incurred following entry on active duty incur interest at whatever rate the servicemember contracts. Charges against a revolving credit account are at whatever rate the account is set up for.

[7] H.R. Rep. No. 108-81, at 39 (2003).

[8] *See infra* App. B.

D. Student Loans

According to the Department of Education (DoE), the six percent interest cap is inapplicable to student loans. [9] The DoE conclusion is based on a section of the Higher Education Act of 1965[10] indicating that federal or state law limitations on the interest rate of a loan do not apply to guaranteed student loans.[11]

This does not mean that relief is not available to students called to active duty from the reserve components or for those who join the armed forces. Although a comprehensive discussion of student loan insurance and the provisions applicable to members is beyond the scope of this publication, it is worth noting that there are some statutory and regulatory provisions which provide for SCRA-like protection. For example, "[a]n institution shall cancel up to 50 percent of an NDSL [National Direct Student Loan] or Perkins loan for service as a member of the U.S. Army, Navy, Air Force, Marine Corps, or Coast Guard in an area of hostilities that qualifies for special pay under section 310 of Title 37 of the United States Code."[12] Additionally, in accordance with the Higher Education Relief Opportunities for Students Act of 2003 (HEROES Act)[13] DoE forbearance[14] rules, which allow for the forbearance on loan repay-

[9] Memorandum, Department of Education, subject: GSL Borrowers Adversely Affected by the Recent U.S. Military Mobilizations (Aug. 29, 1990).
[10] Pub. L. No. 89-329, 79 Stat. 1219 (1965).
[11] 20 U.S.C.S. 1078(d) (LEXIS 2006).
[12] 34 C.F.R. § 674.59 (LEXIS 2006). A servicemember is entitled to a month's worth of special pay for any month that servicemember

(1) . . . was entitled to basic pay or compensation under section 204 or 206 of this title [Title 37 U.S. Code]; and
(2) the member—
   (A) was subject to hostile fire or explosion of hostile mines;
   (B) was on duty in an area in which the member was in imminent danger of being exposed to hostile fire or explosion of hostile mines and in which, during the period the member was on duty in the area, other members of the uniformed services were subject to hostile fire or explosion of hostile mines;
   (C) was killed, injured, or wounded by hostile fire, explosion of a hostile mine, or any other hostile action; or
   (D) was on duty in a foreign area in which the member was subject to the threat of physical harm or imminent danger on the basis of civil insurrection, civil war, terrorism, or wartime conditions.

37 U.S.C.S. § 310 (LEXIS 2006).
[13] Pub. L. No. 108-76, 117 Stat. 904.
[14] "Forbearance means permitting the temporary cessation of payments, allowing an extension of time for making payments, or temporarily accepting smaller payments than previously were scheduled." 34 C.F.R. § 682.211.

ment, are waived for servicemembers[15] on active duty during war time.[16]

III. *Fines and Penalties on Contracts*

50 U.S.C. app. § 523

(a) Prohibition of penalties. When an action for compliance with the terms of a contract is stayed pursuant to this Act, a penalty shall not accrue for failure to comply with the terms of the contract during the period of the stay.

(b) Reduction or waiver of fines or penalties. If a servicemember fails to perform an obligation arising under a contract and a penalty is incurred arising from that nonperformance, a court may reduce or waive the fine or penalty if—

  (1) the servicemember was in military service at the time the fine or penalty was incurred; and

  (2) the ability of the servicemember to perform the obligation was materially affected by such military service.[17]

This section deals with two types of situations. First, when compliance with the terms of a contract is stayed pursuant to the Act, no fine or penalty shall accrue by reason of failure to comply during the period of the stay. Second, when no stay exists and a fine or penalty is imposed for nonperformance, the court can relieve enforcement if the person was in the military service when the penalty was incurred and his ability to pay or perform was materially impaired.

This section can be applicable to late charges on an installment contract, early termination penalties for an automobile lease with an option to purchase clause, or to a delinquency fine on a promissory note. In these cases, the court must conclude that the maker's military service impaired the ability to pay.

IV. *Exercise of Rights Under Act Not to Affect Certain Future Financial Transactions*

This important section was added to the SSCRA in 1991 and remains in the SCRA:

[15] The HEROES Act was obviously designed to benefit servicemembers, but it actual extends to protect a wider group known as "affected individuals" and defined as an individual who—

(A) is serving on active duty during a war or other military operation or national emergency;

(B) is performing qualifying National Guard duty during a war or other military operation or national emergency;

(C) resides or is employed in an area that is declared a disaster area by any Federal, State, or local official in connection with a national emergency; or

(D) suffered direct economic hardship as a direct result of a war or other military operation or national emergency, as determined by the Secretary.

Id., § 5(2), 117 Stat. 906-7.

[16] Notice of Waivers and Modifications, 68 Fed. Reg. 69,312, 316 (Dec. 12, 2003).

[17] 50 U.S.C.S. app. § 523 (LEXIS 2006).

50 U.S.C. app. § 518

Application by a servicemember for, or receipt by a servicemember of, a stay, postponement, or suspension pursuant to this Act in the payment of a tax, fine, penalty, insurance premium, or other civil obligation or liability of that servicemember shall not itself (without regard to other considerations) provide the basis for any of the following:

(1) A determination by a lender or other person that the servicemember is unable to pay the civil obligation or liability in accordance with its terms.
(2) With respect to a credit transaction between a creditor and the servicemember—
    (A) a denial or revocation of credit by the creditor;
    (B) a change by the creditor in the terms of an existing credit arrangement; or
    (C) a refusal by the creditor to grant credit to the servicemember in substantially the amount or on substantially the terms requested.
(3) An adverse report relating to the creditworthiness of the servicemember by or to a person engaged in the practice of assembling or evaluating consumer credit information.
(4) A refusal by an insurer to insure the servicemember.
(5) An annotation in a servicemember's record by a creditor or a person engaged in the practice of assembling or evaluating consumer credit information, identifying the servicemember as a member of the National Guard or a reserve component.
(6) A change in the terms offered or conditions required for the issuance of insurance.[18]

This protection precludes negative fallout from a servicemember's resort to the Act's other benefits and protections. A basic protection would prevent a creditor, for example, from making an adverse entry on a servicemember's credit report because of the reduction in interest on a servicemember's debts to six percent.[19] As one can see, however, there are a number of other protections such as the prohibition against a denial of credit based on utilization of the Act and against discriminatory entries against members of the reserve components.[20] The benefits, in other words, extend to cover more than adverse credit reporting.

[18] *Id.* app. § 518.
[19] *Id.* app. § 527.
[20] *Id.* app. § 518(5). This portion of the statute is very interesting and carries with it an obvious linkage to the Uniformed Services Employment and Reemployment Rights Act of 1994 (USERRA). *See generally* 38 U.S.C.S. §§ 4301-33 (LEXIS 2006). This law works as its name implies: to ensure the continued civilian employment of those who are called to serve the nation through the armed forces. It also works "to prohibit discrimination against persons because of their service in the uniformed services." *Id.* § 4301(a)(3). *See also id.* § 4311.

Of course, creditors may take adverse action against servicemembers who fail to comply with obligations after they are adjusted by reason of the Act. A servicemember who fails to pay monthly installments on an obligation reduced to six percent could be subject to an adverse credit report.

There are several ways to approach the problem when a servicemember receives an adverse credit report because he asserted one the SCRA's stay provisions,[21] the six percent interest provisions, or some other protection. Theoretically, one could institute a proceeding for injunctive or other equitable relief. A better method would be, in certain cases, to file under the Fair Credit Reporting Act (FCRA)[22] provisions for "adverse actions"[23], handling disputed information involving "adverse actions,"[24] and consumer remedies for "willful or negligent noncompliance by credit reporting agencies upon consumer showing of causal connection between inaccurate credit report and denial of credit or other consumer benefit."[25] The definition of what constitutes an "adverse action" is rather broad, "[t]he term . . . has the same meaning as in section 701(d)(6) of the Equal Credit Opportunity Act [15 U.S.C. § 1691(d)(6)],"[26] and defines an "adverse action" as "a denial or revocation of credit, a change in the terms of an existing credit arrangement, or a refusal to grant credit in substantially the amount or on substantially the terms requested."[27] A servicemember who is refused further credit, or has his credit limit downgraded, and so on because of an SCRA assertion could obviously seek relief under this section.

V. *Business and Trade Protection*

One oft overlooked financial protection serves to protect a servicemember's non-trade or business assets if the servicemember is personally liable on the notes from a trade or business:

> 50 U.S.C. app. § 596
>
> (a) Availability of non-business assets to satisfy obligations. If the trade or business (without regard to the form in which such trade or business is carried out) of a servicemember has an obligation or liability for which the servicemember is personally liable, the assets of the servicemember not held in connection with the trade or business may not be available for satisfaction of the obligation or liability during the servicemember's military service.

[21] *See, e.g. id.* app. § 524 (stays or vacation of execution of judgments, attachments).

[22] *See generally* 15 U.S.C.S. §§ 1681-1681u (LEXIS 2006). *See also* ADMINISTRATIVE & CIVIL LAW DEP'T, THE JUDGE ADVOCATE GENERAL'S SCHOOL, U.S. ARMY, JA 265, CONSUMER LAW GUIDE ch. 9, at 30-64 (2004).

[23] 15 U.S.C. § 1681a.

[24] *Id.*

[25] *Id.*

[26] *Id.*

[27] *Id.* § 1691(d)(6). It "does not include a refusal to extend additional credit under an existing credit arrangement where the applicant is delinquent or otherwise in default, or where such additional credit would exceed a previously established credit limit." *Id.*

(b) Relief to obligors. Upon application to a court by the holder of an obligation or liability covered by this section, relief granted by this section to a servicemember may be modified as justice and equity require.[28]

The servicemember's non-trade or business assets are protected while the servicemember is on active duty regardless of whether the military service has materially affected the servicemember's ability to meet the obligation. It seems that the adverse impact of the military service on the trade or business and on the servicemember's ability to meet the obligation is assumed.

[28] 50 U.S.C.S. app. § 596 (LEXIS 2006).

Appendix A

DOJ SSCRA Enforcement

Civil Division

Office of the Assistant Attorney General

Washington, D.C. 20530

March 12, 1991

Honorable Terrence O'Donnell
General Counsel
Department of Defense
The Pentagon
Room 3E 880
Washington, D.C. 20301

Dear Terry:

The Soldiers' and Sailors' Civil Relief Act provides several
important protections for our active and reserve service members
defending the nation's interests. One of these protections is a
maximum interest cap on the financial obligations of individuals
who were subject to an obligation prior to entering on active
duty and whose active duty materially affects their ability to
pay on the obligation. Persons meeting these requirements are
entitled to a 6 per centum cap on the obligation during the
period of active duty.

Most reputable financial institutions are aware of this
provision and promptly give effect to its protections upon
application by the service member. There have, however, been
reports that some institutions are not so cooperative. In the
event an individual service member is denied this protection it
is reasonable to expect that requests may be made for
representation of the interests of these individuals by the
United States. Although the Act does not provide for such
representation, 28 U.S.C. § 517 authorizes the Department to
represent individuals when such representation is in the
interests of the United States. In appropriate circumstances, a
denial of Soldiers' and Sailors' Relief Act benefits would
warrant such representation. By the attached memorandum I have
informed all United States Attorneys of the procedures which
should be used to request representation.

Obviously the Department of Defense shares our commitment to
protect all benefits which Congress has provided for our service
members. In that spirit, I would appreciate your assistance in
disseminating the information and procedures contained in the

- 2 -

enclosed memorandum to appropriate offices within the Department of Defense and its military components.

Sincerely,

Stuart M. Gerson
Assistant Attorney General
Civil Division

U.S. Department of Justice

Civil Division

Office of the Assistant Attorney General

Washington, D.C. 20530

March 11, 1991

MEMORANDUM

TO: All United States Attorneys

FROM: Stuart M. Gerson
Assistant Attorney General
Civil Division

SUBJECT: Requests for Representation Concerning the Soldiers' and Sailors' Civil Relief Act

The deployment of our armed forces to the Arabian Gulf and the extensive reliance upon reservists to meet deployment needs may result in reservists invoking the protections of the Soldiers' and Sailors' Civil Relief Act limiting the rate of interest which they may be charged in certain circumstances. Efforts to realize the benefits of that Act may generate inquiries to your offices concerning the potential availability of representation by the United States in actions to enforce the protections. The purpose of this memorandum is to outline the provisions of the Act and appropriate procedures for processing requests.

The maximum rate of interest provision of 50 USC App. § 526 states:

> No obligation or liability bearing interest at a rate in excess of 6 per centum per annum incurred by a person in military service prior to his entry into such service shall, during any part of the period of military service which occurs after the date of enactment of the Soldiers' and Sailors' Civil Relief Act Amendments of 1942 (October 6, 1942), bear interest at a rate in excess of 6 per centum per annum unless, in the opinion of the court, upon application thereto by the obligee, the ability of such person in military service to pay interest upon such obligation or liability at a rate in excess of 6 per centum per annum is not materially affected by reason of such service, in which case the court may make such order as in its opinion may be just. As used in this section the term "interest" includes service charges, renewal charges, fees, or any other charges (except bona fide insurance) in respect of such obligation or liability.

Accordingly, an individual who was subject to an obligation prior to entering on active duty and whose active duty materially affects his or her ability to pay on the obligation, is entitled to a 6 per centum cap on the obligation during the period of active duty.

Most reputable financial institutions are aware of this provision and promptly give effect to its protections upon application by the servicemember. There have, however, been reports that some institutions are not so cooperative. In the event an individual servicemember is denied this protection it is reasonable to expect that either the Civil Division or United States Attorneys will receive inquiries asking whether the United States may represent the individual. The Act does not provide for such representation. Nevertheless, Title 28 U.S.C. § 517 authorizes the Department to represent individuals when such representation is in the interests of the United States. In appropriate circumstances, a denial of Soldiers' and Sailors' Relief Act benefits would warrant such representation. An individual wishing to request Department of Justice representation concerning this provision needs to submit a signed request through the military department with which the individual served to this office for consideration by the representation committee. The request should include information sufficient to determine the precise nature of the underlying obligation, and how military service has materially affected the individual's ability to meet the obligation. The military department concerned should include its recommendation in a forwarding endorsement.

The Department of Justice views the protection of the benefits of the Act as a very serious matter particularly in this time of reliance on our reserve forces.

Appendix B

Sample Letter to Creditor Requesting Reduction to 6% Interest[1]

[LETTERHEAD]

[Date]

Legal Assistance Office

[CREDITOR ADDRESS]

Dear [Sir or Madam]:

I am a legal assistance attorney writing on behalf of **[CLIENT]**. **[CLIENT]** informs me that [he/she] is currently obligated to your company for a loan bearing an interest rate of [%]. I further understand that this obligation was entered into on **[DATE]**.

Since incurring this obligation, **[CLIENT]** has entered the active military service of the nation in the U.S. **[SERVICE]** on **[DATE]**. This entry into active military service has materially affected **[CLIENT's]** ability to meet this obligation. Under these circumstances, federal law prescribes the maximum interest rate which **[CLIENT]** may be charged.

The Servicemembers Civil Relief Act (50 U.S.C. App. § 527) prescribes a ceiling of 6% annual interest on any obligation under the circumstances described above. This interest rate must be maintained for the entire period that [CLIENT] is on active duty. The percentage cap includes all service charges, renewal charges, and fees. The rate is applied to the outstanding balance of the obligation as of the date of entry onto active duty mentioned above. Any interest charge above this statutory ceiling must be forgiven, not accrued.

Please ensure that your records reflect this statutory ceiling and that any charges in excess of a 6% annual rate are withdrawn. You should also be aware that federal law (50 U.S.C. App. § 532) circumscribes the manner in which you may enforce certain rights under the contract, including any right to repossession of property.

I thank you in advance for your attention to this matter. Should there be any questions, please feel free to contact me at the address above.

Sincerely,

[ATTORNEY NAME]
[RANK], U.S. Army

[1] Legal assistance clients should be advised to send a letter to their creditors shortly before the end of their active service so that the creditor can begin charging interest at the normal rate.

Appendix C

Section Index

50 U.S.C. App. Section	SCRA Section	Name	JA 260 Paragraph(s)
501	1	Short Title	
502	2	Purpose	1-2
511	101	Definitions	2-2
512	102	Jurisdiction and Applicability of Act	2-6
513	103	Protection of Persons Secondarily Liable	3-7
514	104	Extension of Protections to Citizens Serving with Allied Forces	2-7
515	105	Notification of Benefits	1-3
516	106	Extension of Rights and Protections to Reserves Ordered to Report for Military Service and to Persons Ordered to Report for Induction	2-3
517	107	Waiver of Rights Pursuant to Written Agreement	2-5
518	108	Extension of Rights Under Act not to AffectCertain Future Financial Transactions	6-4
519	109	Legal Representatives	2-2
521	201	Protection of Servicemembers Against Default Judgments	3-2, 3-3, 3-4, 3-6
522	202	Stay of Proceedings when Servicemember has Notice	3-5, 3-6
523	203	Fines and Penalties Under Contracts	6-3
524	204	Stay or Vacation of Execution of Judgments, Attachments, and Garnishments	3-8
525	205	Duration and Term of Stays; Codefendants not in Service	3-7
526	206	Statute of Limitations	3-9

50 U.S.C. App. Section	SCRA Section	Name	JA 260 Paragraph(s)
527	207	Maximum Rate of Interest on Debts Incurred Before Military Service	6-2
531	301	Eviction and Distress	4-3
532	302	Protection Under Installment Contracts for Purchase or Lease	4-6
533	303	Mortgages and Trust Deeds	4-7
534	304	Settlement of Stayed Cases Relating to Personal Property	4-6
535	305	Termination of Residential or Motor Vehicle Leases	4-4, 4-5
536	306	Protection of Life Insurance Policy	2-10
537	307	Enforcement of Storage Liens	4-9
538	308	Extension of Protections to Dependents	4-2
541	401	Definitions [Life Insurance]	2-10
542	402	Insurance Rights and Protections	2-10
543	403	Application for Insurance Protection	2-10
544	404	Policies Entitled to Protection and Lapse of Policies	2-10
545	405	Policy Restrictions	2-10
546	406	Deduction of Unpaid Premiums	2-10
547	407	Premiums and Interest Guaranteed by United States	2-10
548	408	Regulations	2-10
549	409	Review of Findings of Fact and Conclusions of Law	2-10
561	501	Taxes Respecting Personal Property, Money, Credits, and Real Property	5-5
562	502	Rights in Public Lands	2-11
563	503	Desert-land Entries	2-11
564	504	Mining Claims	2-11
565	505	Mineral Permits and Leases	2-11
566	506	Perfection or Defense of Rights	2-11
567	507	Distribution of Information Concerning Benefits of Title	2-11

50 U.S.C. App. Section	SCRA Section	Name	JA 260 Paragraph(s)
568 569	508 509	Land Rights of Servicemembers Regulations	2-11 2-11
570	510	Income Taxes	5-4
571	511	Residence for Tax Purposes	5-2, 5-3
581	601	Inappropriate Use of Act	2-8
582	602	Certificate of Service; Persons Reported Missing	2-9
583	603	Interlocutory Orders	3-10
591	701	Anticipatory Relief	4-10
592	702	Power of Attorney	2-9
593	703	Professional Liability Protection	2-10
594	704	Health Insurance Reinstatement	2-10
595	705	Guarantee of Residency for Military Personnel	5-6
596	706	Business or Trade Obligations	6-5